THE LITTLE

Restorative Justice for Campus Sexual Harms

*A Holistic Approach for
Colleges and Universities to Address
Sexual Misconduct and Relationship Violence*

RACHEL ROTH SAWATZKY
MIKAYLA W-C McCRAY

Good Books
New York, New York

Good Books books may be purchased in bulk at special discounts for sales promotion, corporate gifts, fund-raising, or educational purposes. Special editions can also be created to specifications. For details, contact the Special Sales Department, Good Books, 307 West 36th Street, 11th Floor, New York, NY 10018 or info@skyhorsepublishing.com.

Good Books is an imprint of Skyhorse Publishing, Inc.®, a Delaware corporation.

Visit our website at www.goodbooks.com.

Please follow our publisher Tony Lyons on Instagram @tonylyonsisuncertain.

10 9 8 7 6 5 4 3 2 1

Library of Congress Cataloging-in-Publication Data is available on file.

Cover design by Kai Texel
Cover photo by Howard Zehr
Series editor: Barb Toews

Print ISBN: 978-1-68099-917-4
Ebook ISBN: 978-1-68099-930-3

Printed in the United States of America

Contents

Chapter 1: Introduction   1

Chapter 2: Title IX   11

Chapter 3: Restorative Justice in the Context of
Campus-Based Sexual Misconduct   21

Chapter 4: A Collective Wellness Approach to
Addressing Campus Sexual Harms   31

Chapter 5: Practical Action Steps Toward
Implementation   43

Chapter 6: Essential Components of RJ-SM Procedures   59

Chapter 7: RJ-SM Facilitation Best Practices   75

Chapter 8: Campus Climate and Culture   87

Chapter 9: The Promise of RJ for Sexual Harms in
Campus Contexts   97

Resources for Further Learning   103
Endnotes   105

Chapter 1
Introduction

Not everything that is faced can be changed, but nothing can be changed until it is faced.[1]

—James Baldwin

Healers and warriors are not opposites; they are complementaries. Moving beyond binaries, we need not embrace one and reject the other. We can hold them both as one.[2]

—Dr. Fania Davis

The university newspaper features an anonymous letter to the editor outlining a student's experience of reporting a sexual assault to the university. The student writes: "The university doesn't actually care whether or not you have been sexually assaulted. They only care about gaining statistics to claim that we are safe," and continues: "The vagueness of [the university's] response just made me question my character . . . Instead of helping, the questions I received while seeking 'help' made me feel worse about myself."

1

In another situation, a group of students expresses feelings ranging from annoyance to fear as they meet with their club adviser over the increasingly concerning language and behavior of another student, who is very focused on interacting and engaging with them. So far, the interactions have mostly been awkward, irritating, and uncomfortable. However, the content, frequency, and intensity of the advances are starting to feel like sexual harassment, and the student group is beginning to feel anxious and worried about their safety. The students consider their adviser's suggestion to report to the Title IX office (Title IX is federal legislation, designed to protect students from discrimination based on sex and guarantee educational access). However, they are concerned about a potentially biased or disproportionate response because everyone involved, including the student making them uncomfortable, comes from various historically marginalized identity groups. They tell their adviser how the university has responded poorly to similar situations. The students decide against making a Title IX complaint, saying, "We don't want a whole big 'thing,' or for them to get in trouble . . . we just want it to stop." Now the adviser must make the difficult choice about whether to make a report to the Title IX office, with or without the knowledge and consent of the involved students, knowing how that could potentially impact both them and the student causing harm. The adviser also weighs what might happen if they do nothing and feels they do not have any good options.

Another instance involves two queer students who have broken up after dating for some time. At one point after the breakup, the ex-partner pays

2

a drunken visit to the other student's dorm room, where the student and their roommate, a mutual friend, are hanging out. The ex enters the room uninvited, saying they want to discuss the breakup, and an argument ensues. As the situation escalates, the roommate moves to intervene, and the ex hits the other student and their roommate. While the ex continues to yell and throw things around the room, the roommate manages to push them out of the room. The student informs a Residence Director about the altercation and is invited to a meeting with the Title IX coordinator the following week. An investigation is initiated based on the facts of the case, which is very complicated and challenging on a small campus with overlapping friend groups. Instead of an investigation, the student wishes they could have had a safe space to discuss things with their ex.

Title IX Investigative-Adjudicatory (I-A) processes attempt to resolve issues between the individuals directly involved. However, these issues rarely affect *only* those individuals. We engage with one another in interconnected ways—particularly in university settings. The reality is that these cases are complex, dynamic, incredibly disruptive, and often painful for those indirectly involved in what some have called "ripple harms" within communities.[3] Traditional Title IX response methods cannot care for the complex and interconnected ways communities experience impact.

Furthermore, it is impossible to understand or confront sexual harassment without recognizing how structural inequities and intersectional dynamics inform the climate and cultures within which these issues percolate and emerge, resulting in genuine

3

consequences with layered impacts.[4] I-A processes are also challenged to handle the nuances of racism, ethnocentrism, heterosexism, transphobia, and other social inequities that complexify relational dynamics and compound the harms that occur between people, creating (dis)advantages within our institutional systems for different people.

These students and many others are either unsatisfied with or uninterested in traditional Title IX I-A protocols that do not meet their full range of needs. While some individuals may want or need an institutionally facilitated due process resolution to the campus relationship violence or sexual misconduct (RVSM) they have experienced, there is very little data to suggest that I-A resolutions provide satisfactory outcomes for anyone involved.[5] Still, others have experienced actual harm that does not meet the criteria of a Title IX policy violation and are left with little to no recourse. Campus administrators, many of whom are also frustrated with the inadequacy of the status quo, also want a means of taking effective action to address these most challenging campus issues.

Restorative justice (RJ) offers one way forward to begin addressing the array of needs that precede and emerge from situations of campus RVSM. Restorative justice asks: Given the harms, what needs and obligations now exist?[6] RJ for RVSM provides a voluntary and structured way of involving directly affected individuals, including the person harmed (PH) and the person who caused harm (PCH), in a process designed to discern and meet the needs of the PH to the extent possible, given the circumstances, and prevent future misconduct. This is done through

4

a supported collaboration resulting in a resolution agreement that addresses the harmful or prohibited conduct and provides accountability for the harm without formal disciplinary measures against the PCH.

Restorative justice is grounded in a deep wisdom that echoes recognizable values, ideals, and practices of indigenous community cultures worldwide,[7] including Aotearoa New Zealand and a variety of African and Polynesian groups, among others.[8] We offer our humble recognition and deepest gratitude to the groups who claim these traditions and philosophies as part of their people's stories, heritage, or legacy. Our work is further grounded in the wisdom of specific mentors, scholars, and practitioners who have come before us, including sujatha baliga, Angela Davis, Fania Davis, Howard Zehr, and many others.

Our unique backgrounds and perspectives help inform and strengthen our shared concerns and motivations. Growing up as one of six with five brothers of color, Mikayla (Waters-Crittenton) McCray (she/her) witnessed and experienced firsthand the injustices and dangers faced by marginalized groups in the US, from watching a police officer contemplate drawing their gun on her twelve-year-old brother, to the death of her older brother due to institutional violence. Mikayla is motivated to use her words and knowledge to advocate for justice, especially in institutional and systemic contexts. Driven by her passion for restorative justice, Mikayla has dedicated her career to it, from advancing awareness and research around restorative practices in the context of domestic violence, intimate partner violence, and sexual violence, to training staff in facilitation to helping launch a Restorative Justice Diversion program for the city of Charlottesville and Albemarle County, Virginia. Through her work, Mikayla hopes to make justice accessible to everyone, regardless of their background or circumstances.

Growing up in Southern Africa, Rachel Roth Sawatzky (she/her) had an early awareness of significant injustice and its associated trauma, which contrasted with her own White privilege, and she benefited from having role models who heroically demonstrated courage in the face of this evil. These were foundational experiences that have inspired her work over the years: as a social worker in a residential center for sex offenders that incorporated restorative practices into daily routines, and as a foster care and adoption caseworker, assisting children and families impacted by sexual violence. She has also worked within the American higher education arena, holding different student affairs roles and serving as a Title IX coordinator. In this role, she developed a profound appreciation for all that Title IX has done to advance educational access and equity in the US and arrived at the profoundly sobering conclusion that Title IX–compliant responses are often too little, too late or utterly antithetical to what a specific situation requires.

While we offer unique perspectives, we write with a shared voice that emerges from several years as close colleagues and friends, carrying a mutual concern for underrepresented student groups, providing survivors as much agency as possible, and working proactively with a focus on community care. The inception of our restorative justice for sexual misconduct project was in part motivated by several personal experiences that we had as university students ourselves and later as university employees. We have come to see that campus RVSM has devastating impacts, and that there are times when applying Title IX I-A procedures amplifies those harms or creates new ones.

We began our professional collaboration by working on a committee examining policies around sexual misconduct and their impact on student well-being. The committee proposed developing an additional approach to the existing Title IX process that could address the needs that emerge for individuals impacted by campus RVSM. This proposal aligned well with our shared interests, through which some questions emerged: Have our federally compliant institutional policies been asked to do more than they were designed to do in the first place? Are there ways to comply with policy and law *and* be compassionate in addressing the harms and needs that students and others experience because of RVSM? The result was a participatory action research project that led to the development of a draft policy for a specific small liberal arts university, which outlined an RJ-informed, institutionally facilitated set of procedures for responding to specific situations of RVSM. Ultimately, the big-picture goal of these processes was the creation and maintenance of campus communities in which students and others are thriving and fully engaged and there are fewer incidents of what Dorothy Edwards has identified as "power-based personal harm" and more effective institutional responses to RVSM.[9] We discuss this effort further in chapter 8.

The RJ framework challenges the dynamics of the status quo upon which institutions in the United

7

States were established. This includes higher education, which exists because of and perpetuates systems of oppression and marginalization, including white supremacy, patriarchy, and global capitalism. As scholars, practitioners, and now authors, we are committed to holding our institutions to a higher standard. By working within these systems, we are not ignoring these realities but rather aspiring to engage in ways that align with our restorative values and hopes. Zora Neale Hurston reminds us that "if you are silent about your pain, they'll kill you and say you enjoyed it."[10] We recognize the need for continued critique and reform of these systems and commit to using our platforms to elevate marginalized voices and advocate for systemic change. Through our collaboration, we can contribute to a more inclusive and diverse scholarly landscape and help pave the way for future generations of academics, practitioners, and authors to do the same.

This book is written primarily with a United States context in mind, where the frame of reference is Title IX, which specifically prohibits sex-based discrimination in any educational institution that receives federal funding. More broadly, we know that academic institutions worldwide must comply with national laws and institutional policies when responding to sexual misconduct. Regardless of national context, certain things are universal, including that everyone impacted by campus RVSM has various emergent needs related to safety, dignity, and meaningful accountability, which rigid adjudicatory procedures intended to maintain due process often fail to meet.

Those familiar with Title IX can attest that language and terminology will likely change as the law continues to evolve. We use the terms "person(s) harmed" (PH), "person(s) who caused harm" (PCH), "person who has been/experienced harm," and "involved parties" to refer to these individuals. This is for several reasons. First, as noted, these identifiers will likely continue to change as Title IX legislation evolves. Second, we want to use more universally relevant terms to acknowledge an audience both in and beyond the US. Third, we want to lean into a future in which individuals who engage with our campus conduct processes are addressed first as people with nuanced needs and capacities, rather than with terms indicating fixed positionalities (e.g., complainant and respondent). At times, we use the term "sexual misconduct" to identify various types of sexual, gender, and relationship violence because, within a Title IX framework, these harms are considered alleged conduct policy violations. At other times, we use the term "sexual harm" to place particular emphasis on impact. We use the concept of "restorative justice-informed processes" to describe the variety of restorative justice tools and practices that can be used to address specific situations between individuals, attend to community care, and build community, with an eye to the ways that they can influence how we carry out and implement our standard Title IX procedures. On the other hand, "RJ for sexual misconduct" (RJ-SM) is how we reference formal institutionally facilitated restorative justice procedures that complement existing federally mandated minimum procedural processes, otherwise identified as Title IX Investigative-Adjudicatory (I-A) processes in this book.

The scope of this book does not allow for an exhaustive discussion of Title IX history, politics, nuances, RJ philosophy, frameworks, and practices, or a comprehensive litigation of the appropriateness or effectiveness of RJ in cases of campus RVSM. However, these are critical and foundational components of the discussion. Chapters 2 and 3 offer grounding in Title IX basics and an overview of fundamental RJ principles and values. Chapter 4 offers an ideal "whole campus approach" that emerges from a public health model and a framework of tiers to develop an RJ program. Chapters 5 and 6 outline program development and implementation action steps and the essential procedures within an RJ-SM offering. Chapter 7 explores best practices for RJ-SM facilitators, and chapter 8 discusses the critical role of institutional climate and culture in program development and implementation. Chapter 9 closes the book with encouragement for the journey. Each chapter includes a "Case in Point," a scenario that emerges from our experiences as practitioners.

This book explores possibilities for developing and implementing RJ-informed procedures in response to campus RVSM. While this is not a "how to" manual, we hope that it is a practical and accessible primer for college and university administrators interested in exploring RJ's possibilities, and in doing so offer more effective responses to harm and move our institutions toward greater levels of social justice.

Chapter 2
Title IX

Justice, then, is not dependent upon the law. That a society does not outlaw an activity does not mean that the activity is just . . . The more we act for the common good, by being inclusive and letting others speak for themselves, the more we can learn about the people whom we ought to become.[1]

—James Keenan, SJ

B ecause you picked up this book, it is likely that your current institutional responses to relationship violence or sexual misconduct (RVSM), even those that comply with policy and laws, are not doing enough to help those who experience sexual harm on your campus. Our status quo response methods are not very nimble or able to attune to situational nuance, including the variety of individual, collective, and cultural identities we have and the ways they overlap to shape our experiences in the world.[2] This is because the standard policies and procedures for these situational nuances need frameworks and tools to meaningfully address the causes and effects of these harmful situations as well as to address

11

individual and collective responsibility, which Title IX does not. This chapter unpacks these realities, with an overview of Title IX legislation, its retributive framework, how institutional policies and procedures typically work, and its limitations, for which RJ may serve as a corrective.

A Basic Overview of Title IX

Title IX of the Education Amendments Act of 1972[3] was the first comprehensive US federal law to prohibit sex discrimination and protect civil rights and equal access based on sex in educational programs and activities. The original intent of Title IX was to ensure that educational environments are free from sex- and gender-based barriers to academic access and achievement in recruitment, admissions, financial aid, and educational rules and regulations (including housing and facilities, graduation criteria, athletics, health and wellness care, educational employment, and committees). Through this law, the US government has used its regulatory power to mandate gender equality and consciousness in the US education system.[4] By these measures, there is no doubt that Title IX has made a significant positive impact since its passage in 1972, and it remains essential for institutions to comply with its guidelines to prevent and address sex discrimination and protect the academic interests of students and others in campus contexts.

A university's Title IX policies specifically define and prohibit sexual assault, sexual and gender-based harassment, and stalking, among other behaviors and conditions. All university faculty, staff, students, and third parties are protected by the policy and responsible for their conduct under the provisions of the policy, which applies to issues occurring within the university's programs and activities in a defined geographical context. If a school receives federal funding, it must (1) ensure equal opportunity to participate in education programs and activities, which are to be free from all forms of sexual misconduct and sex- and gender-based discrimination, and (2) maintain institutional policies that outline transparent and fair procedures for responding promptly to known instances of sexual misconduct and discrimination and then remedy the resulting adverse effects.

Over the past fifty-plus years, Title IX regulation and guidance have evolved into strictly formulaic, highly litigious, "quasi-judicial" investigative processes administered locally by colleges and universities.[5] Like criminal justice procedures, these response mechanisms are adversarial and intended to maintain due process for all involved. However, they are not criminal or legal, even though they can feel and sound that way. There are investigators and witnesses, and attorneys may be involved. At the time of this writing, hearing processes require an opportunity for cross-examination. However, Title IX I-A processes are institutional, designed to address potential and specific policy violations, not legal proceedings or other processes that might address specific harms. A significant development occurred in 2020, when regulations changed to allow colleges and universities to begin offering more customizable, institutionally facilitated "informal" responses to campus sexual misconduct, specifically including mediation and restorative justice among the potentially viable options.

Title IX's Retributive Framework

The generally understood central agenda of higher education in the US is to increase student agency and facilitate personal development, growth, and learning. Theoretically, the primary purpose of Title IX—to remove barriers to education—would seem in alignment with these concerns; however, the lived reality of standard Title IX policies suggests different priorities. Emphasis tends to focus on which policies have been violated, who committed the offense, and what consequence is deserved. This aligns with the criminal/legal world's retributive framework, which asks what law has been broken, who broke the law, and what they deserve as a consequence (Figure 1).[6]

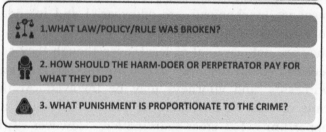

RETRIBUTIVE JUSTICE FRAMEWORK

1. WHAT LAW/POLICY/RULE WAS BROKEN?

2. HOW SHOULD THE HARM-DOER OR PERPETRATOR PAY FOR WHAT THEY DID?

3. WHAT PUNISHMENT IS PROPORTIONATE TO THE CRIME?

Figure 1

When a retributive approach is used in response to campus misconduct, individuals are disempowered[7] and prevented from accessing their agency, thus stunting growth, learning, and development, which is antithetical to the larger project of higher education[8] and contrary to what we know about the cognitive and psychosocial development of college students.[9] In a standard Title IX process, both the PH and the PCH are disempowered.[10] For example, the university adopts surrogacy for the PH as their decision-making ability narrows and shifts to the institution administering the response. Ironically, while the assumption of control and capacity is experienced as institutional over-functioning, it simultaneously under-functions in not providing the protections or services that community members trusted or expected to be in place. The harm of the original incident is exacerbated when this happens. Further hurt and disillusionment layer over the original harm that led to engaging university conduct mechanisms in the first place,[11] amounting to what is known as "institutional betrayal."[12] By the end of the process, everyone involved is typically exhausted and frustrated.

Standard "Status Quo" Title IX Procedures

A snapshot overview of a standard procedure goes as follows (Figure 2). When a so-called "complaint" of a potential policy violation is made to the Title IX office, a prompt and equitable response is required. First, the report is reviewed to assess whether the allegations could be a potential policy violation based on the type of behavior, who is involved, where it occurred, and the context in which it happened. Based on the answers to these questions, an investigation is initiated in which all involved parties are interviewed, evidence is collected and assessed, and an investigative report is issued. Following this, there is a hearing in which an independent adjudicator considers the investigative report, relevant testimony, and evidence to determine if a policy violation(s) occurred. After a finding of "responsible" or "not responsible" is issued according to the institution's standard of proof—e.g., Preponderance of the Evidence (50 percent or more) or Clear and Convincing (100 percent)—a written "notice of hearing outcome" is issued to the involved parties. If applicable, remedies and sanctions are determined, and then optional rounds of appeals processes follow.

Figure 2

The Inadequacy of the Status Quo

Unfortunately, Title IX has proven a less than suitable response to sexual harm, struggling to appropriately and adequately meet the needs of individuals impacted by sexual misconduct. Policy definitions and standardized procedures repeatedly fail to prevent such misconduct, address its causes, or remedy its effects. Ironically, every Title IX coordinator will say that what impacted parties want is precisely that—an institutionally facilitated process that will stop the behavior and prevent it from happening again. However, these same coordinators will also agree that it is very rare for parties to resolve a complaint through a status quo process and be satisfied with the outcome.

Some of this is because Title IX's fundamental design follows the criminal legal system's retributive model, which is intended to maintain due process, undoubtedly a crucial democratic concept. Yet, several shadows are associated with it. First, a "fair" process often feels very unfair and weighted against the person who has alleged harm against them. On principle, Title IX coordinators, investigators, and hearing officers are motivated to act with intentionality and care, but their attempts to maintain a position of neutrality toward situations are unfortunately perceived by involved parties as indifferent and failing to attend to the need to be seen and believed.[13]

Second, due process requires a decision based solely on the presented evidence. So often the specific details surrounding a potential Title IX violation are unclear and subjective, with exact recall influenced by the impacts of trauma and other layered aspects of identity and experience. It is challenging and sometimes impossible to determine precise details and gather enough concrete evidence to meet any standard of proof. Moreover, since findings are based on standardized criteria, they may only address some unique circumstances in each case. And so, students and others who encounter a university Title IX process because of their experiences of RVSM report inappropriate, inadequate, unhelpful, or mishandled responses by the institution.[14] Process outcomes feel variously irrelevant, too lenient, excessively harsh, or even retraumatizing, depending on the individual's point of view and experience. This compounds the traumatic impacts of what has led them to engage the process in the first place.

17

All of this leaves university Title IX and compliance offices with an image problem. They are typically viewed as untrustworthy and must deal with public misperceptions of their intentions and integrity. The inappropriateness or inadequacy of the procedures, coupled with misunderstandings of complicated nuances of ever-evolving laws and associated policies and the (at times necessary) lack of institutional transparency in a given case, leads to anger, or at least bewilderment. The applicability and relevance of the policy to specific situations and confusion about reporting obligations of various university faculty, staff, and administrators can result in what one faculty member identified as a feeling of being "flummoxed."

It turns out that prescribing a single path to resolving misconduct, such as prescriptive Title IX I-A processes, is generally unhelpful, as these approaches fail to attend to the real issues that precipitate sexual misconduct and are too rigid and limited to meet the multiplicity of engendered needs, ultimately leaving the parties unsatisfied with the outcomes. This disservice to the parties ironically exposes the institution to liability. Furthermore, it interferes with the goals of education to develop autonomous, responsible, reflective, and critically engaged members of society. What is needed are more comprehensive and holistic solutions that meet federal requirements, address harms, and are consistent with educational goals. Institutions and their people need law and policy, but in cases of sexual misconduct, those who have experienced harm need something different or additional. In university settings, we must meet federal law requirements and then go further, comprehensively addressing misconduct, remedying its effects, and attending to the needs and harms of impacted individuals and the conditions in which the misconduct happened to prevent its recurrence.

A Case in Point: Frankie and August Part 1

August is a second-year resident assistant (RA) who meets first-year resident Frankie, a person on the autism spectrum, on move-in day.[15] Over the semester, Frankie enjoys getting to know many new friends, especially his RA. He begins going out of his way to see August on campus and by mid-semester has become increasingly persistent, regularly waiting outside her room to talk to her and getting up early to see her in the cafeteria where she works the breakfast shift. August starts changing her sleep schedule to avoid bumping into Frankie in the residence hall and changes her work schedule as her discomfort with the attention increases. At a Halloween residence hall social, Frankie approaches August and attempts to kiss her without consent. August is very upset by the encounter and decides to talk to the Title IX office. August tells the Title IX office that she does not want anything "bad" to happen to Frankie or for him to get in trouble. She only wants him to understand that his behavior is unacceptable and to stay away from her. The Title IX coordinator issues a "no-contact" order and begins an investigation. Living in the same building, having only one dining option on campus, and with overlapping social circles, the no-contact order soon feels very cumbersome for both parties and even their friend groups. Frankie and August both feel embarrassed about the situation, albeit for different reasons. Ironically, August feels like she has been sanctioned for making a report, while Frankie, confused about what the issues are, is under a lot of stress, worried that he will make another misstep. The investigation is exhausting for everyone. Eventually, August comes back to the Title IX office to ask if she can drop the issue or if, at the very least, there is another way to deal with the situation because she feels on edge, distracted, and disengaged. We will return to Frankie and August's story at the end of the book.

Chapter 3
Restorative Justice in the Context of Campus-Based Sexual Misconduct

The moral arc of the universe bends at the elbow of justice.[1]

—Dr. Martin Luther King Jr.

Restorative justice is about relationships and how we create, maintain, and mend them when harm is done. It is based on a philosophy of interconnectedness, revealing how our actions affect others because we exist in relationship with each other, as epitomized in the Zulu word "ubuntu," which roughly translates as "I am because we are; and since we are, I am complete."

This is the motivation of a diverse community of global practitioners who employ unique skills, practices, and tools grounded in the restorative justice philosophy, many of whom work throughout higher education, especially within student affairs disciplines.

In this chapter, we outline how this relational approach to justice can be applied to cases of sexual misconduct (RJ-SM), common RJ-SM processes, and

21

building blocks for RJ-SM within Title IX process. In doing so, we have attempted to walk the delicate line between being stuffy, overprotective, or paternalistic about restorative justice and being too casual or "playing fast and loose" in approaching this work in the context of sexual misconduct.

RJ-SM's Restorative Building Blocks and Framework

RJ-SM represents a paradigm shift from how institutions have traditionally responded to sexual misconduct under Title IX. RJ-SM is built on restorative building blocks (Figure 3), emphasizing civility and courtesy and focusing on addressing the harms and needs of the stakeholders who are directly impacted with a goal of healing and repair through voluntary and collaborative processes.

RESTORATIVE JUSTICE BUILDING BLOCKS
Zehr, 2015

EMPHASIS	CIVILITY & COURTESY, MAKING THINGS RIGHT TO THE EXTENT POSSIBLE
FOCUS	ADDRESSING HARMS & NEEDS
GOALS	IDENTIFYING OBLIGATION & PROCESSES TO REPAIR HARM
PROCESS	VOLUNTARY, INCLUSIVE, COLLABORATIVE, ITERATIVE
STAKE-HOLDERS	IDENTIFYING OBLIGATION & PROCESSES TO REPAIR HARM

Figure 3

The restorative justice building blocks structure responses to the impacts of harmful behavior, or the conditions that created it, by responding to seven prompts (Figure 4). The first three prompts allow the PH, the PCH, and any others who are directly involved to name the impacts of the experience and determine the necessary measures and actions required to achieve the maximum possible resolution (harms, needs, and obligations). Prompt four invites input on how to structure an RJ-SM process, as flexibility in meeting needs is vital to ensure that obligations are met. Finally, harm does not happen in a vacuum; there are ripple impacts on the community. Questions five, six, and seven encourage collaboration around the underlying causes of the harm and how to secure a future where similar issues are prevented.

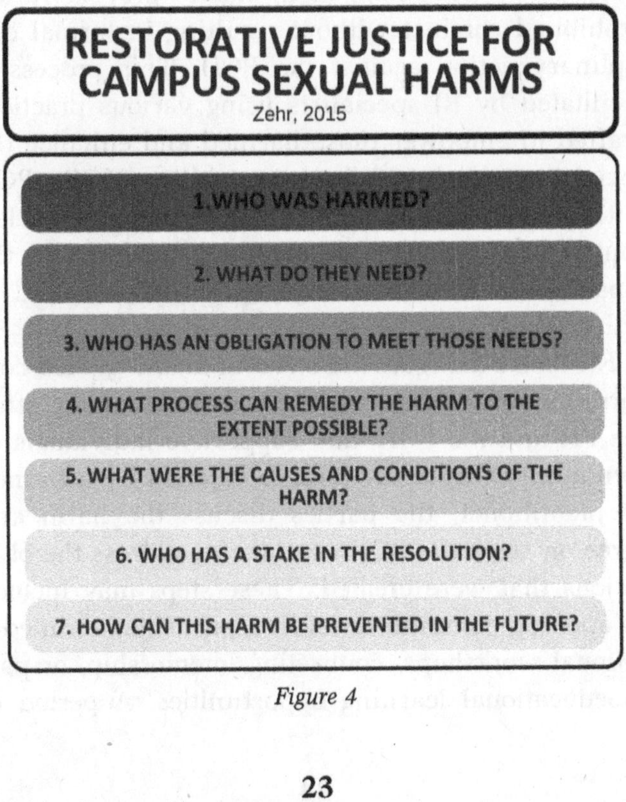

RESTORATIVE JUSTICE FOR CAMPUS SEXUAL HARMS
Zehr, 2015

1. WHO WAS HARMED?

2. WHAT DO THEY NEED?

3. WHO HAS AN OBLIGATION TO MEET THOSE NEEDS?

4. WHAT PROCESS CAN REMEDY THE HARM TO THE EXTENT POSSIBLE?

5. WHAT WERE THE CAUSES AND CONDITIONS OF THE HARM?

6. WHO HAS A STAKE IN THE RESOLUTION?

7. HOW CAN THIS HARM BE PREVENTED IN THE FUTURE?

Figure 4

This contextual component pairs well with Title IX, which expects universities to assess and address safety and climate relative to any issue to reduce the possibility of harm recurring, including considering how policies and procedures can be amended to enhance the safety and welfare of their students, faculty, and staff.

Common RJ-SM Practices

Restorative justice applied in the Title IX context is a voluntary, supportive, structured, and collaborative process between directly impacted individuals, which results in the development of a resolution agreement to address the harm, to the extent possible, given what happened, and to prevent future prohibited conduct without resulting in formal disciplinary action against the PCH. This process is facilitated by RJ specialists using various practices crafted to empower those harmed and enhance the social engagement and accountability of the PCH within the community.[2] Facilitated dialogue, circles, shuttle negotiation, and surrogacy are some of the most common restorative justice processes used in universities.[3]

Facilitated dialogues are structured and guided conversations involving two or more individuals, often the PH and the PCH, and supportive individuals or community members. With facilitation by a trained RJ practitioner, the parties discuss the harm and agree on steps the PCH can take to address the obligations that were created. These steps may include an apology, community service, participation in educational workshops, counseling, mentorship, or psychoeducational learning opportunities. A period of

24

voluntary leave, perhaps until the PH has graduated, is a possible outcome that the parties may consider. Facilitated dialogue can happen between individuals, for example through victim-offender dialogue, and within groups through community conferencing or family group conferencing, among other models.

Like facilitated dialogue, *circles* usually include those directly involved and may also include others who were secondarily impacted, along with support people. In these structured conversations, again facilitated by a trained practitioner, each person can respond to several carefully crafted questions that explore the impact of the harm and ideas for addressing the resulting needs and obligations.

Shuttle negotiation involves the RJ facilitator communicating with the PH, PCH, and others affected. The facilitator shares information and conveys questions between the parties. This indirect facilitation does not require face-to-face meetings between the involved parties. An approach that has been successful in higher education contexts is using *impact statements* written by the PH and shared with the PCH as part of the shuttle negotiation or as a stand-alone tool or experience. Another use for shuttle negotiation is as preparation for facilitated dialogue and circles. If it meets everyone's needs and results in an agreement, the process may successfully conclude without a face-to-face conversation.

Surrogacy is a dialogue practice used when one of the parties does not want to be directly involved in the process or with the other party. In these situations, a surrogate, often someone who has experienced similar harm as the PH or who has caused similar harm as the PCH, serves as a substitute for one party or the other to facilitate understanding of the impacts of the harm.

Implementing these practices varies across institutions. Universities need to approach these practices thoughtfully, considering the needs of the individuals involved, their specific local context, and relevant legal requirements. Additionally, utilizing well-trained facilitators and ensuring the well-being of all participants are crucial for the success of RJ-SM (see chapter 7 for more detail).

RJ-SM: A Corrective-Additive to Title IX

Restorative justice in the case of sexual misconduct can serve to correct some of the concerns with and limitations of Title IX I-A protocols. First, Title IX operates on the principle of due process, whereas RJ-SM operates with "multi-partiality." Multi-partiality involves equitable alignment with everyone involved to guide a collaborative approach. This means that individuals are less likely to feel isolated and more likely to feel seen and heard, thus mitigating the potential loss of personal agency.

Second, some of the most frustrating Title IX I-A cases involve actual forms of harm that do not "rise to the level" of a Title IX policy violation or are situations where the available evidence does not justify a finding of responsibility according to the standard of evidence. The person(s) harmed have no recourse, leaving impacted parties in a vacuum. RJ-SM can serve as a procedural additive and be immensely helpful in these cases, providing a facilitated way forward. RJ-SM is forward-looking and constructively focused on impact and need, instead of backward-looking at proof of violation and "justifiable" punishment.

Third, where I-A protocols are often confusing and complicated and result in outcomes that are perceived as variously irrelevant, too heavy-handed, or wholly inadequate, RJ is transparent, iterative, flexible to the situation at hand, and adaptable to the needs of those involved.[4]

Fourth, people who have experienced some form of campus RVSM will often express that they are not interested in a long, drawn-out investigation that may or may not accomplish anything meaningful. Instead, they simply want the negative behavior to stop. Depending on the type of issues and the individuals involved, they may also want the responsible person/ people to understand the negative impacts of their behavior. In these cases, RJ-SM can be very helpful. As a participatory and collaborative approach, the likelihood of the institution's involvement causing additional harm is mitigated, and the possibility for long-term healing, meaningful accountability, and learning increases. While not a panacea, RJ-SM assumes the ability to learn and grow, thus aligning with the developmental tasks of traditionally aged college students to become conscientious, autonomous, and productive citizens and contributors to their chosen fields. Because sexual harms involve the removal of agency and control, RJ-SM processes also make practical sense by returning control to the impacted individuals and capitalizing on their agency to find ways forward.

Restorative justice can and should address general conduct issues and RVSM in campus contexts. Individuals who have experienced RVSM within institutional contexts, including the students whose stories opened this book, have various needs that align with a set of "restorative values" including safety, support, collaboration, empowerment, voice, choice, and an acknowledgment of, or accommodations for, a variety of personal and cultural dynamics. Underpinned by the principle of "nothing about me without me," restorative justice-informed response mechanisms to campus RVSM can theoretically offer all these things, emphasizing civility, inclusivity, and reflective action in addressing genuine problems and needs through collaborative partnerships with those most directly impacted,[5] through tailored and flexible responses that result in more satisfactory outcomes for those who have experienced harm.

A Case in Point: Alex and Taylor

Alex has been accused of nonconsensual sexual activity with Taylor at a concert venue off campus. Taylor reports the incident to the Title IX office, which determines that it can be referred to the RJ-SM team. First, Taylor and then Alex are willing to try an RJ-SM process. A member of the RJ-SM team contacts both parties separately to explain RJ and the voluntary nature of participation, emphasizing that the aim is to address the harm caused and offer accountability for the harm caused. Alex and Taylor consent to participate, and the facilitator meets individually to discuss their perspectives on the situation, their feelings about the situation since it occurred, and what they would like to see happen as a resolution. The facilitator also assesses their emotional preparedness for the facilitated process and the possible resolution options.

Taylor requests a facilitated dialogue, which involves Alex, Taylor, and the support people they choose. Taylor shares their perspective on the incident and its impact, saying that since the episode they have been questioning their judgment and whether the situation happened as they remember it. Specifically, they want to understand what Alex was thinking at the time. Alex responds by saying that they honestly thought Taylor was okay with what was happening and that they did not realize that there was a problem until they got a notice from the Title IX office, at which point they felt confused and scared. Alex then acknowledges the harm the situation caused and shares what they have thought about since. With the facilitator's guidance, Alex and Taylor develop a written agreement outlining that Alex will participate in personalized one-on-one coaching sessions to support the development of skills that promote consensual and safe intimate relationships and sexual behaviors. (This is provided by a trained staff person at the university's sexual assault prevention and advocacy center. At another university this may be offered by the student conduct or Dean of Students' office or a community anti-violence non-profit.) The RJ-SM team provides support, as needed, while Alex carries out the agreement. The team meets with Taylor to assess any ongoing needs and to address emerging requests for counseling and connection to a survivor support group. At a designated time the RJ-SM team contacts Alex and Taylor to ensure that both parties are satisfied with the process and its outcomes.

Chapter 4
A Collective Wellness Approach to Addressing Campus Sexual Harms

Without reflection, we go blindly on our way, creating more unintended consequences, and failing to achieve anything useful. [1]

—Dr. Margaret J. Wheatley

Our attention now shifts to the organizational context in which restorative justice for sexual misconduct (RJ-SM) occurs by locating it within a broader educational model prioritizing collective, holistic well-being, known as the "whole campus approach," which emerges from the world of public health. Applying a public health model to a higher education context emphasizes community welfare through a focus on prevention, education, and population-level strategies to improve overall campus well-being and resilience in the face of challenges. It does this by identifying and then addressing the root causes of problems with a three-pronged approach of assessment, prevention and education, and intervention.

31

Prong One uses *assessment* measures to track health and look for patterns to determine and analyze the effectiveness of interventions. That information helps develop policies and guidelines that incentivize individuals, and even departments or service units to begin making healthful choices on both a proactive and an ongoing basis to support the development of more extensive organizational conditions that can sustain well-being over the long term. Prong Two involves *prevention and education* efforts to promote health and wellness, address risk factors, mitigate concerns before they begin, and empower individuals to make informed and healthy choices. Prong Three involves *community-level interventions* and strategies that tackle health issues across larger community groups.

Whole Campus Approach

In an educational setting, a public health approach translates into a comprehensive "whole campus approach," often conceptualized with three tiers of intervention that focus on preventing issues at their

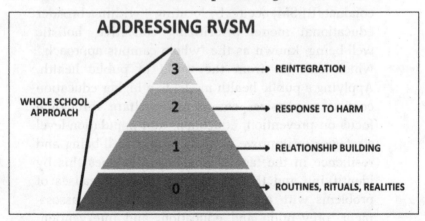

Figure 5

root and considering the overall well-being of the educational community: Relationship Building (Tier 1), Resolution Responses (Tier 2), and Reintegration (Tier 3).[2] We propose an additional layer of intervention, a "Tier 0," focused on Routines, Rituals, and Realities. We will look at each tier to make this model of addressing campus RVSM operational, noting that an RJ-SM program would nest in Tier 2.

Tier 0: Routines, Rituals, and Realities

This substructure grounds the relationships within our organizations (Tier 1), shapes responses to harm (Tier 2), and informs learning, growth, and change (Tier 3). Tier 0 considers institutional habits and regularities, traditions, and facts on the ground against factors relating to institutional/unit health and well-being, such as the restorative values of civility, agency, freedom, transparency, and collaboration named at the close of chapter 3. Like Prong One of the public health model, tasks in this tier include assessing and analyzing organizational structures and practices to understand specific strengths, challenges, and opportunities that can occur through climate assessments, data analysis, policy evaluation, as well as reimagining institutional routines and rituals, reviewing student conduct and human resources procedures, evaluating community and affinity building activities, and reexamining communication practices to align with restorative values.

If the goal is to go big at Tier 0, it is necessary to activate the interest and buy-in of informed leadership, especially those who possess the personal competencies to create and nurture institutional norms, routines, and rituals that resist power-based personal harm. This looks different at each institution but involves leadership at any level, ideally the most senior leaders. These leaders:

- Communicate practically and efficiently.
- Authentically honor the inherent worth and contributions of others.
- Expect that people will listen to each other.
- Value diverse perspectives.
- Are committed to shared learning and collaboration.

With such leadership, campus communities become characterized by psychological safety, which in turn facilitates learning and growth; fosters a willingness to raise concerns, make mistakes, and try new things; and encourages innovation and creativity. When leaders actively promote and support Tier 0 initiatives, it signals a commitment from the top, which then influences the entire organizational culture and climate. A favorable climate subsequently encourages the development and implementation of policies that promote restorative values.

However, Tier 0 skills and practices can be activated by individuals at any university level with restorative values applied before, beyond, or throughout the implementation of Tiers 1–3, offering accessible entry points for integrating RJ-informed practices throughout the university ecosystem. For example, one university may follow the tiered structure, strategically mapping a context-appropriate approach to Tiers 1, 2, and possibly Tier 3. Another university, instead of codifying things, may plan to disperse restorative justice values and practices for general use in the campus community, strategically increasing the resiliency of the university's structures. While work at Tier 0 is optional for implementation at Tier 1 and beyond, those campus communities that lay a Tier 0 substructure are well prepared to launch Tier 1 plans if, and when, their communities call for that.

Tier 1: Relationship Building

Where Tier 0 emphasizes leadership and the organizational routines and broader realities, Tier 1 centers on improving interpersonal skills for individuals within campus community subgroups. According to the public health model, Tier 1 seeks to prevent harm through education and training as well as the establishment of shared values that invite the authentic engagement and holistic welfare of each member to optimize the well-being of the educational community. RJ suggests that this is made meaningful by creating or enhancing relationships and affinity.

While folks can always hone and sharpen their skills and develop new competencies, Tier 1 does not necessitate formal facilitator training or practitioner experience (nor does Tier 0). Anyone—students, staff, or faculty—can bring restorative practices into student government operations, the classroom or laboratory, a department, division, or center, or a faculty or board of directors meeting. Regardless of the context, when people engage in open-hearted ways, it can have unforeseen rippling impacts. Tier 1 activities involve opportunities to foster and strengthen connection and community. This might include carefully structured discussions for different student cohorts and affinity groups, as well as for faculty, staff, and administrators, on topics relevant to their specific roles and conducted in ways that honor various identities and experiences. Opportunities for authentic engagement can be meaningful and transformational. For example, faculty are eager to discuss how they can help create inclusive classroom and research environments, staff want to share their experiences and brainstorm solutions to feeling underappreciated and overworked, and graduate students are keen to think with their colleagues about how various aspects of their identities influence their experiences in labs, fieldwork, and getting appropriate credit for their research. Other topics for these groups may include power dynamics, how sex and gender influence our day-to-day interactions in working and learning environments, and other factors that impact unit climate. Meanwhile, in addition to frank and respectful discussions about consent and how alcohol and other drugs correlate to sexual violence, undergraduate students benefit from conversations that help them think about and name their values and how those translate in interactions with others, including in their sexual relationships. These conversations, which can follow a traditional circle format[3] or a facilitated dialogue model,[4] allow campus community members to share their concerns openly and authentically, thereby collaboratively setting explicit normative standards for their particular community subgroup and building relationships and community affinity (for more, see chapter 3).

An additional Tier 1 entry point may be to experiment with holding a regular student organization, administrative staff, faculty, or board meeting using a circle format. For example, a circle process structures a regular Monday staff meeting after a Friday departmental retreat. The first circle round may invite each

36

person to share something that they enjoyed about the retreat; the next circle round could allow people to articulate something that they might change about the retreat; and in the final circle round, everyone can share something that they will continue to think about or take with them from the retreat. In subsequent meetings, team members can prepare and lead a circle to process an issue or event, build camaraderie and community, or honor and celebrate someone or something. This practice can make a small but significant shift to shared leadership and restorative values in group interactions. In sharing the responsibility and expectations around circle preparation and leadership, each person can express their ideas, practice how they show up in space, and learn how to cultivate meaningful engagement for and with others. While the supervisor or manager might typically run team meetings and set the agenda, this is one small piece that everyone can participate in, which can help shape team culture with more equitable power sharing.

Beyond subgroup, classroom, or large group iterations, many education and training opportunities can be encouraged at Tier 1 to develop skills—e.g., accessibility-related issues, bystander intervention strategies, and dynamics related to equity issues for BIPOC, women-identifying, and LGBTQIA+ community members. Additionally, offering approachable Title IX and RJ-SM policy review sessions that prioritize honesty and transparency, and invite engagement on how the policy applies within the community's lived experience, are essential as basic prevention building blocks and trust-building exercises at this tier.

Tier 2: Resolution Responses

RJ-SM facilitated processes are situated in Tier 2 because of their goals for accountability, learning, growth, safety planning, and personal healing. In this tier, an RJ process offers individuals who are engaged in an institutional process addressing alleged misconduct an alternative to an I-A process, which can amount to a challenging investigation and formal hearing on the one hand, or an inadequate or inappropriate process on the other. Those involved in the incident collaboratively design customized responses, such as shuttle negotiation or facilitated dialogues. These processes may also go beyond the individuals immediately affected, as the impacts of such incidents often reach wider campus communities. Additionally, these measures are not limited to interpersonal harm; they can also include restorative actions to address incidents that have a broader adverse impact on the campus climate or within units and departments that have experienced ripple harm because of an incident. The following chapters look at Tier 2 RJ-SM institutionally facilitated responses to harm in detail.

Tier 3: Reintegration

Tier 3 involves institutionally facilitated procedures to structure the reintegration of the person who caused harm to the educational community after a removal, absence, or other consequence outlined in an RJ-SM process resolution agreement. While a Tier 1–3 approach has been modeled at elementary and middle school levels,[5] fewer schools have done so at the high school level,[6] and even fewer have done so at the college and university level, offering much room for innovation within higher education.

This gap is because the Tier 3 task of reintegrating a student found in violation of a campus sexual misconduct policy is so delicate, requiring vulnerability, humility, trust, and transparency from all parties involved—qualities that tend to be in short supply within higher education.

Institutions are using several promising practices in developing Tier 3 programs.[7] For example, at one university, a group of student leaders began a student advocates initiative, resembling student-led restorative justice councils at other institutions where students navigate conflict using a peer-to-peer model. In this case, the model is student-led, run, and driven, so with the support of a faculty adviser and the freedom to be creative, they developed something that would work within their community context and lived experience as students.

On the other end of the formality scale, some universities are offering Circles of Support and Accountability (CoSAs) which embody a restorative model grounded in a highly successful approach to overseeing the reentry of sex offenders from prison.[8] Campus CoSAs engage trained volunteers who consistently meet with returning students, providing social support to aid in their successful graduation to monitor and address any early warning signs of reoffending to reduce risk.[9] Another model uses personalized one-on-one psychoeducation coaching sessions to support the PCH in cultivating wellness-focused attitudes and skills that promote consensual and safe intimate relationships and sexual behaviors using a curriculum that is individually tailored for each participant based on their self-identified values and goals.[10]

While a whole campus approach may be the big picture, long-term plan, it could be overwhelming to start there. Even if you did jump in the deep end, a whole host of preparatory things would have to happen to lay the groundwork. Ideally, a strategic plan to offer Tier 2 RJ-SM is developed on a foundation of Tier 1 approaches and Tier 0 preparatory work. Depending on various situational campus dynamics, however, some schools will assess their need and readiness to be limited to Tier 0 and/or Tier 1 strategies. Others are prepared to offer Tier 1 and, eventually, Tier 2 incident response mechanisms. Ideally, Tier 2 and 3 are developed simultaneously so that a successful Tier 2 process can offer the PCH meaningful options for learning and reintegration. A tiered approach is phased, highly customizable, adaptable, and responsive to the needs and readiness of the community. It is also able to be employed in various US, cultural, and broader global contexts and can be scaled according to various aspects of capacity and resources.

A Case in Point: Faculty Climate Concerns

It comes to the attention of the chair of a relatively small department that their faculty need help to be collegial with one another. There is tension in the room at faculty meetings, and people are reluctant to engage in departmental extracurriculars, such as new student recruitment activities. During regular check-in meetings with several junior and newer faculty members, it becomes clear that the climate of the department is unhealthy, including when concern is registered about the unequal distribution of administrative tasks, dismissive attitudes toward female colleagues, and when folks are excluded from decision-making processes in situations that impact their work.

The chair knows that a hostile climate can quickly impact culture by undermining morale, positive engagement, and efforts to recruit quality students and faculty. The chair contacts the Title IX office to report what they learned, but because none of the complaints amount to a policy violation, the Title IX office cannot follow up with any formal institutional processes. Instead, they make a referral to the RJ-SM team. This team suggests a series of restorative interventions, customized to the needs of the department. The first is leadership coaching with the chair to support her in following up with specific faculty performance reviews in which expectations are clearly named. Second, the team consults with the chair on thoughtful communication to the department that is as transparent as possible about the issues, clearly offers information about support resources, and invites community involvement in a series of circle processes related to the climate concerns and to address specific harms (a Tier 2 response). Finally, the RJ-SM team facilitates sessions within the department to address specific cultural vulnerabilities that are impacting overall health, using a model through which participants identify positive aspects and challenges of their community culture.[11]

Across these responses, individuals who have been specifically impacted feel that the harm they have experienced is seen and acknowledged. Individuals' feelings of isolation on the one hand and group failure on the other are relieved. The department identifies a more balanced understanding of their internal dynamics and is given opportunities to foster connection and compassion with one another, inspiring a renewed sense of hope for their collaborative work moving forward.

Chapter 5
Practical Action Steps Toward Implementation

I am no longer accepting the things I cannot change.
I am changing the things I cannot accept.[1]
—Dr. Angela Davis

We advise campuses to approach their RJ-SM implementation project with careful consideration and common sense, resisting the urge to get ahead of themselves based on their level of readiness. We also urge optimism, engagement, and giving things a try, particularly at the Tier 0 and Tier 1 layers. This chapter focuses on implementing a Tier 2 RJ-SM program, one step at a time, with encouragement to start slowly and think creatively.

The following suggestions emerge from our own learning experience and revolve around five steps:

1. Examine and assess institutional values and readiness;
2. Staff and invest in the program;

3. Make sure that the design and details of policy and procedures are integrated into existing ones;
4. Collaborate and communicate across campus to ensure a smooth implementation process;
5. Implement the new process and evaluate the results.

The final suggestion is to start slowly and be creative. We will take each of these suggestions in turn.

1: Examine and Assess

The process of developing a Title IX policy amendment to include an RJ-SM resolution pathway can be approached following the restorative framework:

1. What are the educational community's needs?
2. What structures and processes could address those needs?
3. Who are the stakeholders with an investment in seeing that these needs are addressed and that we improve our processes moving forward?

Inviting the wisdom of the community, who ultimately have a stake in the outcome of the development of an RJ-SM policy, may be less efficient than designing something with a small team. However, the end product will have more integrity and be much more contextually appropriate as a result. For example, including the voices of queer students, staff and faculty, BIPOC community members, first-year undergraduate students, graduating seniors, and graduate students is a powerful statement about institutional commitment to restorative values. Moreover, it is vital to include input from people who have experienced harm, specifically those who have been through a Title IX process, and people who have caused harm or have been found responsible for violating the institution's Title IX policy in the past.

To that end, the first step toward implementing a Tier 2 RJ-SM program is testing the idea for feasibility with a cross-stakeholder interdisciplinary task force to consider institutional values and readiness for development and implementation (Task Force 1). Task Force 1 might comprise representatives from the Title IX office, academics, retention services, and various student affairs offices (including conduct and housing), representing various personal identity groups to the extent possible. Additionally, athletics, multicultural and international student services, and graduate and undergraduate student representatives can be valuable partners in this effort.

Task Force 1's first job is to review written and unwritten institutional values and assess their alignment with restorative values. The second job is to examine how these principles are expressed or at least compatible (or not) with various conduct policies and procedures, including those designed to respond to RVSM. This is done to honestly appraise what kind of lift developing an RJ-SM will require. If restorative values are entirely antithetical to institutional values and norms, it will be a different project than if the campus already embraces principles that align with restorative justice. To do this examination, the task force may consider, for instance, academic integrity policies; statements of student rights, responsibilities, and expectations; human resources policies; and institutional procedures for responding to sexual misconduct for faculty, staff, and students. Through an honest appraisal of facts on the ground, this initial multidisciplinary evaluation serves the additional purpose of securing stakeholder awareness and buy-in. The third priority for Task Force 1, with the potential addition of some carefully identified administrative liaisons, is to determine if the university administration is ready to take any perceived liability and reputational risks needed to go beyond tacit approval or politically correct rhetoric into practical realities in launching an RJ-SM program. This means securing adequate and meaningful institutional buy-in and investment right out of the gate.

After feasibility has been confirmed, a second task force (Task Force 2), composed of the campus restorative justice practitioners and representatives from the Title IX office, is primarily tasked with the policy development phase. Task Force 2 reviews relevant law and federally mandated institutional policies and procedures, looking for quick wins in ways the latter can be adjusted or implemented more restoratively. This also clarifies the additional Tier 2 RJ-SM procedures that could supplement the current Title IX I-A procedures beyond minimum compliance standards. Depending on campus dynamics, additional participants on Task Force 2 could include representatives from the dean of students' office, human resources office, office of the ombuds, general counsel, and consultant experts from outside the university who can offer a more objective perspective on the issues.

> **Examine and Assess Considerations**
> * Are the institution's articulated values and mission merely rhetorical and aspirational, or relevant to realities on the ground?
> * How compatible are the institutional values and mission with restorative values?
> * Do institutional processes reinforce institutional values and align with the mission?
> * What tier is the most appropriate starting place for the context?
> * What are trust levels in *current* conduct processes among faculty, staff, and student groups?
> * Are there ways that *current* procedures and processes can be supplemented, scaffolded, and bookended with restorative principles and practices, and/or is a distinct RJ-informed institutional policy and procedure called for or appropriate at the institution?
> * What practical information sharing needs to happen to proactively address potential misinformation and/or concerns that could derail the rollout later?

2: Staff and Invest

Often, an initiative like this is launched because an individual or small group becomes aware of the powerful potential that restorative justice holds for meaningfully addressing RVSM. They elect to learn all they can and influence others to do the same. To be sure, initiating an RJ-informed approach to address sexual misconduct is a project that requires personally invested champions, but that will not be enough to get something like this across the finish line. RJ-SM is effective when capably developed and facilitated by well-resourced and trained university personnel. This requires the endorsement and support of university administration, tangibly represented by allocating resources in staffing and otherwise upfront at the visioning and pre-implementation stages.

The primary staff structure requires a director or coordinator-level position that leads the RJ-SM team. This individual offers additional perspective and serves to consult with facilitators throughout processes. Additionally, the team includes at least one facilitator who provides direct service with the PH and PCH, and ideally more than one facilitator, offering representation of various identities and mitigating potential conflicts of interest concerning involved parties. If RJ-SM is an innovation that an existing team is expected to implement, it is important to invite their honest reflection on their current capacity levels for doing something new, different, and potentially additional to work they are already responsible for. Ensuring that the team is entirely on board, feels well-equipped, and is prepared to be innovative and collaborative is critical to success. We also emphasize how imperative adequate team training is in various subject areas, such as Title IX policy and how RJ-SM fits into that, and skill building in the administration of the RJ procedures, responding to disclosures, and motivational interviewing, among others.

If RJ-SM is to be a legitimate offering alongside Title IX I-A processes, it will be equally resourced in terms of endorsement, staff, monetary resources, and training. If boosting current staffing levels is necessary, the university's commitment to supporting this initiative can confirm that this is a manageable mandate over the long term and not the extra uncompensated work of a few individuals. While it may not be feasible or necessary to balance Title IX and RJ-SM staff at the outset, the eventual goal should be parity between the number of RJ-SM staff and Title IX intake specialists, investigators, and outcomes coordinators, if it is to be an equally legitimate offering. Furthermore, the unit needs to be connected to the appropriate university departments in ways that advance the work, with full authority to do the work, and with the necessary endorsement of university leaders, from the president to the provost, to the Title IX office, to student affairs, to human resources.

> ### Staff and Invest Considerations
> - What is the current level of staff capacity for innovation and collaboration?
> - What are current staff excited about, and what do they need when they think about being involved in a new RJ-SM program?
> - What is the staff structure of current Title IX I-A processes?
> - What is the appropriate and necessary staff structure for an RJ-SM program initially and in an ideal future?
> - How will the program be resourced to get from here to there?
> - Where will the RJ-SM program sit organizationally? What needs are met, and what problems are solved by its placement on the organizational chart?

3: Design and Detail

As indicated, it is imperative that the Title IX coordinator officially sanctions the use of RJ-SM and that it is explicitly outlined in the Title IX policy. In other words, the existing sexual misconduct policy should be amended to include RJ-informed procedures and a rubric to determine the situations in which it can be used as a resolution option. Additionally, RJ process referral, intake, case procedure, closure, and documentation processes should be detailed with opportunities for customization to each situation based on the needs of the individuals involved.

When a high-level draft of the RJ-SM policy and procedures is prepared, we recommend having the university general counsel review the draft to ensure coordination with institutional Title IX procedures and compliance with current state and federal law. We make this suggestion with the awareness that not all general counsel offices will support restorative justice generally and/or its application to campus sexual misconduct specifically. If the general counsel and other potential gatekeepers can understand how restorative justice makes sense from a practical perspective, they are more likely to lend their support. This includes understanding that investment in time, infrastructure, and other resources on the front end will gain efficiencies in the long run through, for example, higher rates of participant satisfaction with the process and resolution and increased feelings of institutional affinity for the various stakeholder groups.

Understanding that each campus needs to determine the most politically expedient path forward, the idea is to give gatekeepers such as the general counsel's office every reason to support the effort. That may look like gauging the idea of a full-fledged program with trusted general counsel and stakeholders first and then proceeding cautiously, starting with more modest goals, gaining small wins, and presenting that evidence in support of a proposal to go bigger based on early successes to relevant influence leaders. Alternatively, it may be best to proceed with optimism and hope, asking for forgiveness later if needed!

Design and Draft

- Are precisely detailed RJ-SM procedures written into existing Title IX policies?
- Who are the critical decision-makers on campus?
- Has/should the general counsel review the draft policy and procedures?
- What information do critical decision-makers need to support this project?

4: Collaborate and Communicate

Whether a phased whole-school approach or a focused Tier 2 RJ-SM initiative, coalition-building and partnership are imperative throughout the development and implementation process. In terms of collaboration and communication, the Title IX office is the primary partner since they will be involved in offering RJ-SM as a legitimate option and referring cases to the option when it is selected by the PH. Additionally, we suggest continuing to cultivate a collaborative alliance with the partners on Task Forces 1 and 2 who could be helpful campus ambassadors ahead of and throughout implementation. Some additional offices to work with through the implementation stage include the sexual assault advocacy and prevention office(s), services for students with disabilities, Greek life, ombuds offices, and the faculty and staff senates, in ways that make the most sense for the campus. Nurturing and leveraging these collaborative partnerships ahead of and throughout the roll-out of the RJ-SM program will provide a significant advantage in the successful launch of the program.

At various points, there will need to be some practical and proactive information-sharing of the benefits of the approach, addressing any potential misinformation and/or concerns from within the institution that, if not addressed, could derail the initiative's rollout. There might already be general (negative) assumptions about restorative justice, Title IX, HR, and/or the student conduct office within the institution. It is essential to be aware of these assumptions and actively work to clarify unrealistic expectations and any misconceptions. As we know, lack of transparency, or the perception thereof, can lead to institutional betrayal. Getting a feel for what students, faculty, and staff believe about the policy is just as important as being clear about what the policy is and is not and what kinds of steps will be taken in keeping with the policy. Perception is often reality and word spreads fast, so everyone must be on the same page. The first student, disaffected alum, faculty, or staff person who feels unsupported and betrayed by the institution will likely share that with whomever they feel needs to know that information. Then, there will be other hurdles to overcome.

> ### Collaborate and Communicate
> - Who are the critical campus partners and stakeholders that must be fully aware of this policy and procedure and how it may benefit constituents?
> - What is the communication or marketing plan for this new way of responding to RVSM, and how will those who need to know be notified?

Transparency is also necessary for the policy itself. It is essential to have a prominent place to display RJ-SM resources to ensure students and others know what to expect, what is possible, and what will and will not happen. Offer easy-to-follow flow charts, graphics of various kinds, and short policy and procedure videos that are as uncomplicated as possible, accessible in plain language, and thoughtful of the needs of students and others who may be interested in utilizing this approach. Offer policy and procedure review sessions customized to the audience with scenarios and small group discussion opportunities in faculty and staff meetings throughout the year. Beyond these basic ideas, think creatively about customizable approaches that can foster transparency related to RJ-SM, if not Title IX processes as a whole.

5: Implement and Evaluate

With the preceding four steps completed, it is time to develop a comprehensive and appropriately timed implementation strategy. This will look different for each campus based on available staff capacity and financial and other resources. A potential implementation timeline might be sketched as follows:

- Summer: Examine and assess institutional values and readiness.
- Fall term: Staff and invest in the program.
- Winter term: Make sure that the design and details of policy and procedures are drafted to be integrated into existing ones.
- Summer 2: Collaborate and communicate across campus to ensure a smooth implementation process. Offer policy and procedure review sessions customized to the audience with engagement opportunities in stakeholder meetings throughout the year.
- Fall term 2: Implement the new process and evaluate the results.

Reflecting on implementation successes and learnings through informal and formal program evaluations is also vital to offer participant constituents the opportunity to provide valuable feedback on the process. This can be done with the support of the university's Institutional Research Office, as well as through internal program evaluation tools. See the Resources section at the back of this book for some starting points. Over time, the use of rubrics for referral and intake processes offer helpful frameworks for evaluating the overall effectiveness of RJ-SM as an additional procedural option to the standard Title IX I-A process, allowing for analysis of trends and patterns among cases that can lead to a fine-tuning of the rubric itself and, by extension, the RJ-SM process. We look at rubrics in more detail in chapter 6.

Start Slow, Be Creative

A comprehensive whole-school approach or even a targeted focus to develop a Tier 2 structured RJ-SM program may not be possible. Instead, a campus may only be ready to dip a toe in the RJ-SM water. In these situations, a great way to begin is to start slowly by evaluating the current federally mandated and/or other required institutional procedures to determine ways to supplement, scaffold, and bookend the existing protocols with restorative values and practices before and until a fully developed RJ-SM policy and procedure can be added to the menu of formal options. An RJ-informed I-A process invites the individual parties to consider who has been harmed and/or impacted, what their needs are, and whose responsibility it is to address those needs and in what way on a case-by-case basis, even though that goes beyond what Title IX strictly expects of the parties involved. In other words, consider who has been harmed or impacted, what their needs are, and whose responsibility it is to address them, and then, get as creative as possible in developing solutions to address those questions. Beginning this way also allows scaling and customization of a program for a particular setting. There are many opportunities for this type of restorative augmentation, from team-specific efforts to more extensive university-wide interventions, beyond Title IX and student conduct offices, to focus on adding or shifting what we already (must) do where possible to support restorative values. Ultimately, this basic formula can address many things, from broader institutional, cultural, and climatic dynamics to addressing levels of individual impact from harm. Getting started at all may mean starting slowly and inviting a kind of creativity where we ask people the right questions and try to find ways forward together.

A Case in Point: Chris and Jamie

A university staff member, Chris, has been accused of gender discrimination by their colleague, Jamie. Jamie alleges that Chris consistently makes disparaging comments, repeatedly fails to use Jamie's pronouns, excludes Jamie from significant professional opportunities, and generally creates a hostile work environment based on gender. Jamie makes a formal complaint to the Title IX office.

While there has been some interest in a whole school approach and specifically a Tier 2 RJ-SM for the whole campus community, faculty governance structures, union regulations, and limited staffing is hampering program development and implementation. In the meantime, RJ-SM is being piloted in staff cases. The Title IX office notifies the university's human resources department and both offices review and assess the case as suitable for an RJ-SM process. Chris and Jamie are willing to participate voluntarily, and the case is referred to the RJ-SM team.

The facilitator meets individually with Chris and Jamie for pre-conferencing to explain the process and its objectives, after which they both provide informed consent to participate. Over a few weeks, pre-conferencing continues with each party to identify desired outcomes and to assess emotional preparedness for a facilitated dialogue, the method the parties choose to reach a resolution agreement. Through Jamie and Chris's facilitated process, Jamie shares about the chronic work stress, hypervigilance, social isolation, and feelings of alienation from colleagues that they have experienced as a result of the misgendering. Chris is not ready to legitimize Jamie's concerns entirely, but their perspective softens and they can acknowledge that Jamie has been harmed.

With the facilitator's guidance, Jamie and Chris create a written resolution agreement outlining specific actions that will reestablish a feeling of connectedness for Jamie, encourage personal growth for Chris, and pave the way for organizational improvement to foster a gender-inclusive workplace. First, Chris apologizes in writing and commits to participating in training sessions to learn more about diversity. Next, department leadership agrees to support the development of an employee resource group focused on gender inclusivity, where employees can share experiences, offer support, and contribute to organizational initiatives. As a result of this group's efforts, leadership agrees to review the equal opportunity employment and anti-discrimination and harassment policies, establish department-level inclusive language expectations, adopt an inclusive dress code that does not enforce gender-specific norms, and offer regular professional development opportunities on a variety of diversity-related issues for all employees. They also begin conducting regular assessments of diversity and inclusion practices within the department for continued improvement over time.

Chapter 6
Essential Components of RJ-SM Procedures

There is no power for change greater than a community discovering what it cares about.[1]
　　　　　　　　　　　　—Dr. Margaret J. Wheatley

A restorative justice resolution option for sexual misconduct supplements the I-A procedural pathway mandated by Title IX. As a supplement, RJ-SM can be employed to satisfy institutional Title IX requirements by augmenting existing frameworks, rubrics, and criteria and creating new ones to guide RJ-SM options. After a Title IX intake assessment and subsequent referral from the Title IX office to the RJ-SM team, an RJ process addressing campus relationship violence or sexual misconduct (RVSM) involves (1) an RJ-SM intake; (2) pre-conferencing; (3) a facilitated process; and (4) the resolution agreement (see Figure 6). After briefly introducing three core RJ-SM criteria, this chapter explores each of the procedural components, including policy considerations for assessments and referrals.

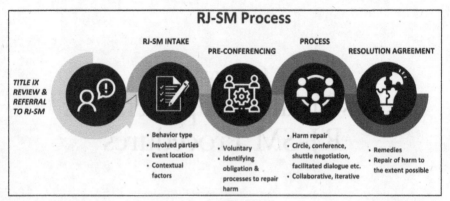

Figure 6

RJ-SM Hallmark Criteria

Several RJ-SM hallmark criteria require a brief introduction before looking at procedures, as they ground decisions made at various points in the process. First, RJ may not be possible in all campus sexual misconduct cases, particularly where allegations indicate certain forms of Title IX policy violations. Federal and state law and university policy will indicate the types of cases that are eligible for referral for RJ-SM. Second, the PH and the PCH must give voluntary consent to participate and actively engage with an authentic intention to repair harm. With flexible processes, the facilitator continually obtains feedback from those involved about what is working and what is not working, as well as why, when, and how the facilitated process can be attentive to their needs. Finally, RJ-SM requires a baseline recognition of the general substance of the harm caused and experienced, even if there is no agreed-upon narrative or a capital-T shared "truth" agreed to by all involved. These criteria are discussed in more detail later in this chapter and chapter 7.

Title IX: Intake Assessment

Here is an example of a standardized Title IX intake process for cases that may be eligible for RJ-SM. When a PH notifies the Title IX office about a potential policy violation, their case is processed by staff members who have a robust understanding of both Title IX and RJ-SM procedures (and see the value of RJ-SM) and have specialty training in trauma-informed interviewing, receiving disclosures, and anti-racism and implicit bias. Because the intake team, and the Title IX coordinator who reviews all RJ-SM referrals, are the gates through which cases pass to reach a restorative process, RJ-SM and standard I-A processes must be outlined and offered with equal confidence, mitigating any bias to the extent possible.

In all cases referred for RJ-SM, the Title IX coordinator reviews a certain level of anonymized documentation to determine whether the case must be addressed by the Title IX office and if it is eligible for I-A, RJ-SM, or both. Intake is guided by a referral rubric (discussed below). Due to federal mandates, the Title IX coordinator has the final say on whether a case indicating a possible Title IX violation is eligible to be routed to the RJ-SM team. If approved, the designated intake personnel meets with the PH to see if they want to initiate the RJ-SM process. When the Title IX intake with the PH is complete, consultation can begin with PCH, with whom procedural options are also outlined. Both parties then agree to an RJ-SM process.

Intake staffing is an important consideration and is informed by a number of local campus factors including state and institutional political dynamics and institutional sensitivities and priorities. Potential intake staffing configurations include, but are not limited to:

- Designee from the Title IX office handling all intakes;
- Designees from both the Title IX and RJ-SM offices conducting intakes together;
- Designee from a confidential campus resource, such as an advocacy office, handling intakes;
- Designee from a confidential campus resource and a designee from the Title IX office handle all intakes together.

Each campus will need to determine what makes the most sense given its institutional structures and existing staffing models while prioritizing equity, transparency, and other restorative values.

Cases that originate in the Title IX office and constitute an alleged Title IX policy violation will initially be reviewed by the Title IX coordinator. However, RJ-SM processes do not *have* to originate in the Title IX office. If a process starts in the RJ-SM office or is referred directly from another campus partner, for example human resources or the dean of students' office, then the intake assessment and rubric start and continue from the RJ-SM office.

Referral Rubric: From Title IX to the RJ-SM Team

Rubrics outline the specific expectations and criteria for a case to be considered suitable for a particular resolution process, helping all the parties involved

62

understand what is required for their case to move forward in a specific way, and mitigating the potential for unmet expectations to arise later in the process. A rubric also enhances transparency in the decision-making process; clearly defining the factors considered when determining the appropriateness of a resolution process allows all parties to understand the basis on which decisions are made. Some leading complaints about Title IX processes are how confusing they are and how long they can take. A clearly outlined rubric supports efforts at transparency and improves efficiency, streamlining the assessment process and allowing decision-makers to assess cases more efficiently, and reducing the likelihood of oversight or unnecessary delays. Different cases may be better suited to specific processes, including I-A or RJ-SM, and a rubric helps ensure that the chosen process aligns appropriately with the nature of the issue and the goals of those involved. Finally, using a rubric facilitates communication between parties and decision-makers, fostering more open and constructive dialogue.

Of utmost importance, rubrics standardize criteria for referring cases in ways that guard against bias and help ensure that referral decisions are made as objectively and consistently as possible. One of the necessary criteria in any social justice work, which we believe RJ-SM advances, is the reduction of Racial and Ethnic Disparities (RED).[2] Time and time again, when individuals make decisions about who is and is not eligible for a process, decisions almost always fall along racial and ethnic lines, so creating as many safeguards against bias as possible is critical. If the Title IX office or larger institutional structures cannot or will not ensure safeguards against RED and bias, implementing RJ-SM is not recommended. No matter what the intentions, not having these safeguards in place can cause more harm.

Additional Intake and Referral Considerations: Title IX

Several additional considerations need to be evaluated concerning intake and referrals. First, consider any relevant institutional policies that need to be assessed for their compatibility with an amended Title IX policy that includes RJ-SM. For example, some institutions may have a policy that limits how many infractions can be processed at any one time using a given process or may have policies guiding the order in which various sorts of potential policy violations are addressed.

Another important consideration is the clear and careful communication methods and protocols that need to be in place between Title IX and RJ-SM teams, especially regarding intakes and rubrics. Lots can go wrong when offices do not have the appropriate communication mechanisms in place or take inadequate care in passing information back and forth between themselves, in communication with academic departments, sports teams, supervisors, witnesses, support people, or other parties adjacent but not directly involved in the case. It is essential to develop the most efficient, effective, and transparent communication methods possible, while also honoring the dignity and privacy of the parties involved. Title IX and RJ-SM teams must be open enough with each other and those with a "need to know" status to maintain transparency, efficiency, and mitigate community "ripple harms," and be careful to clarify what should/must be shared beyond immediately impacted individuals and how those individuals would like that ideally done. This is especially necessary if the institution has a policy of reporting to law enforcement behavior that carries potential criminal liability. In this way, agency and privacy are honored. When Title IX offices offer RJ-SM as a resolution option, it expands choice for the PH and supports their healing journey. It can also increase the likelihood of positive outcomes for the PCH through the assistance of personal and institutional networks that support the PH and PCH. Maintaining choice, autonomy, and agency for the PH and the PCH throughout an RJ-SM process can be delicate but is imperative.

RJ-SM Intake Assessment
Once a case has met the criteria for RJ-SM referral from the Title IX coordinator, the RJ-SM team will complete their own intake and assess that the case is appropriate and ready for RJ-SM, participants are ready, and a facilitator is prepared and trained to support the process (Figure 7).

While RJ-SM procedures are customizable and adaptable to the particulars of a case and the needs of the folks directly involved, there is also a need for some procedural uniformity. This provides an opportunity to review logistics such as the communication preferences of the PH and PCH, again prioritizing agency and privacy, outlining what to expect before, during, and after the process and what may or may not be possible along the way. This procedural uniformity also allows for negotiating logistics (e.g., facilitation model, who will be present, how seats should be arranged), and documenting each party's consent to participate, which are all important administrative

65

components of a facilitated RJ-SM process. These initial meetings also offer an opportunity to review the social, emotional, academic, and other support systems already in place for each party as the process progresses.

An RJ-SM intake rubric includes assessment of specific criteria and factors, many of which are equivalent to the Title IX referral rubric, and which align with the restorative values:

1. Voluntariness—The PH and PCH are willing to participate in a restorative justice process, and neither party is coerced or pressured into participation. It can be challenging to nuance the pros and cons of an RJ-SM process with each party when one of the outcomes is not having the PCH's disciplinary record affected. However, the voluntary nature of RJ is a fundamental principle.

2. Informed consent—Securing informed consent ensures that the PH and PCH fully understand and want to participate in the restorative justice process.

3. Safety—Potential safety concerns have been assessed and those concerns can be adequately addressed within the RJ-SM process. The PH's emotional, mental, and physical safety must be centered throughout the processes.

4. Equity—The RJ-SM process can be carried out equitably for all parties involved, considering power dynamics, identities, and other relevant factors. This is a particular

issue in cases involving employees, where differing roles can create challenging power dynamics in employee/employee situations and employee/student situations. However, safeguards can address power and contra-power dynamics. There is no inherent reason why individuals in different positions of power cannot participate together in a restorative justice process. However, the institution will need to make decisions about it deliberately.

5. Support—Support structures, such as counseling services, are available for both the PH and PCH during and after the RJ-SM process. RJ facilitators are not therapists. If the mental health of either party will impact their ability to participate as fully as possible, it will not be possible to proceed.

6. Training—The qualifications and training of the RJ facilitators or coordinators who will be involved in the process are adequate.

Other elements of a RJ-SM intake rubric include:

7. Alignment—Whether the RJ-SM process aligns with Title IX regulations and institutional policies. For example, are the severity and specific nature of harm (e.g., harassment or assault) suitable for a restorative justice approach according to federal and state law and institutional policy?

8. History—Whether previous incidents or disciplinary history of the involved parties precludes their involvement in an RJ-SM process by institutional policy.

9. Timeline—Whether the proposed RJ-SM process timeline aligns with the university's goals for resolution.
10. Confidentiality—Whether the RJ-SM process upholds confidentiality and privacy for the parties involved.
11. Impacts—Whether the RJ process can address potential ripple impacts within the university community.

In developing an RJ-SM intake rubric, it is important to note that collaboration with experts in Title IX compliance, restorative justice practitioners, and other relevant stakeholders is vital. Additionally, the rubric must be reviewed regularly and updated to reflect evolving best practices and legal considerations and the latest federal Title IX regulations, or their equivalent.

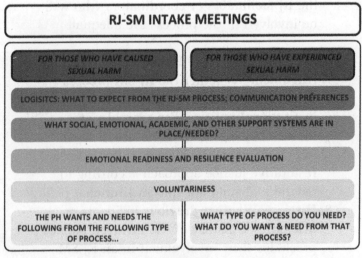

Figure 7

The RJ-SM team will initially, and throughout the facilitated process, assess the following:

- Multi-partiality—The qualifications and training of the RJ facilitators or coordinators who will be involved in the process and their ability to remain multi-partial in each case.
- Responsibility—The PCH's willingness to accept some responsibility for harm caused even if a standard narrative cannot be established.
- Collaboration and confidentiality—If the parties can engage collaboratively to develop a path forward to repair the harm with respect for confidentiality in the process.

These steps segue into more thorough preparations for any facilitated interactions between the parties. This includes evaluating all parties' emotional readiness to handle and navigate the process. The assessment may cover a range of emotional competencies and factors, including an ability to recognize and understand their own emotions and how emotion impacts thoughts and behaviors; the capacity for emotional regulation and impulse control; the ability to handle stress and challenge; the capacity for empathy; a certain level of emotional resilience in the face of challenge, ability to effectively express emotion, and capacity to listen to and understand the emotions of others; their approach to challenges and conflicts; and whether they are capable of a solution-oriented mindset.

Once the RJ-SM team accepts a case, the RJ-SM process begins. This process includes three stages: pre-conferencing, an RJ process, and a resolution agreement.

Pre-conferencing

After the intake process has concluded, additional preparatory work, typically called "pre-conferencing," is conducted in separate discussions with each party. Through pre-conferencing, the needs and ideal outcomes of the PH and PCH are identified, and rapport and trust are built. Additional pre-conferencing may be guided by a set of restorative questions (Figure 8). These questions help the facilitator gauge the parties' state of mind both at the time of the event and since it happened as well as their current needs, helping to determine when a facilitated process will take place and what that will look like.

RESTORATIVE QUESTIONS

FOR THOSE WHO HAVE CAUSED SEXUAL HARM	FOR THOSE WHO HAVE EXPERIENCED SEXUAL HARM
WHAT HAPPENED?	
WHAT WERE YOU THINKING AT THE TIME?	WHAT DID YOU THINK WHEN YOU REALIZED WHAT HAD HAPPENED?
WHAT HAVE YOU THOUGHT ABOUT SINCE?	WHAT HAS THE HARDEST THING BEEN FOR YOU?
WHO HAS BEEN AFFECTED BY WHAT YOU HAVE DONE? IN WHAT WAY?	WHAT IMPACT HAS THE INCIDENT HAD ON YOU (AND OTHERS)?
WHAT DO YOU NEED TO DO TO MAKE THINGS RIGHT?	GIVEN WHAT HAS HAPPENED, WHAT DO YOU NEED TO MAKE THINGS AS RIGHT AS POSSIBLE?

Figure 8

RJ Process

During the pre-conferencing process, with the support of the RJ-SM facilitator, the parties decide which restorative approach or model they will use. This may include one of the approaches outlined in chapter 3, such as facilitated dialogue or a restorative circle, shuttle negotiation, circle of accountability, some combination of these, or a different model that suits the needs of the parties. The RJ-SM facilitator will lead this process accordingly.

Resolution Agreement

The resolution agreement is a set of mutually agreed-upon steps for repairing harm and preventing its recurrence. This signed document represents the culmination of the facilitated process between the PH and PCH. Successful agreements are SMART: specific, measurable, achievable, relevant, and time-bound.[3]

If the case was originally an alleged Title IX policy violation, the Title IX coordinator approves the resolution. After the resolution is approved, it is signed by all parties and the matter cannot be shifted to a different resolution path (i.e., a Title IX I-A resolution process). The institution will not "re-adjudicate" the issue, and no further disciplinary action is pursued against the PCH. This standard ensures that the involved parties can have confidence in the integrity of the RJ-SM process. Following the conclusion of the formal facilitated process, a member of the RJ-SM and/or the Title IX office monitors completion of the resolution agreement.

Additional RJ-SM Process Considerations

Either party may discontinue an RJ-SM process and shift to an I-A resolution process up to the point of signing the final RJ-SM resolution agreement. In this case, the Title IX I-A process starts all over again, as any information obtained during the RJ process cannot be used in any other university or legal process. Based on campus culture, other institutional policies, and relevant state laws, schools need to make some additional decisions, including, for example, any conditions for direct dialogue between PH and PCH and what happens to the issue if a resolution agreement is not able to be reached, or is reached but not completed. Also, institutions need to determine which restorative practices and tools will be offered as part of their RJ-SM processes, and if any restorative practices might be made available after a Title IX I-A resolution process—e.g., sanctioning circles after a judicial hearing board or hearing officers' determination of responsibility or Circles of Support and Accountability (CoSAs) for students reintegrating into their campuses following a period of exclusion.

Evaluation mechanisms *must* be in place for case review, and to integrate information and lessons learned into processes for the future—e.g., what is working well and where there can be improvement to ensure a positive experience for everyone involved. At minimum, evaluation criteria mirror the intake rubric by assessing: voluntary participation, attention to safety concerns, support resources, equity, and consideration of power dynamics, identities, and other relevant factors. Institutions may wish to add other variables or experiences to evaluate. Facilitators also benefit from the opportunity to reflect on their experiences with other colleagues through case debriefing, including an assessment of the facilitator's ability to remain multi-partial in each case.

A final note on autonomy, choice, and self-determination related to RJ-SM processes: throughout the intake meetings and pre-conferencing, voluntariness is assessed on the part of all parties. In a Title IX I-A process, things can proceed with or without the involvement of either or all parties.[4] Additionally, in Title IX, the PCH is never expected to accept responsibility; in fact, the PCH has the opportunity to argue their *lack* of responsibility. By contrast, an RJ-SM process requires the PCH to acknowledge the impact of the harm, even if they cannot or will not recognize their specific role or responsibility. The focus here is on creating containers for issues that are safe enough for accountability, rather than perpetuating an environment where denial and minimization of responsibility prevail. This means that "voluntariness" carries a slightly different weight and obligation for the PCH. It is thus necessary to lead with compassion and respect for what is at stake for each participant. We talk more about autonomy and agency in chapter 7.

A Case in Point: Rae and Von
Two students, Rae and Von, have been dating for approximately nine months and live in the same residence hall. While standing on the steps of their residence hall, an argument ensues in which Rae pushes Von, who falls down the steps. Both students are upset, and Von makes a formal complaint to the Title IX office. An intake team member meets with Von to assess their needs and interests and to review I-A and RJ-SM process options. The Title IX coordinator then receives the de-identified intake document and then uses the rubric to determine that the case is eligible for a RJ-SM referral. After Von indicates interest in an RJ-SM process, the Title IX office reaches out to talk with Rae to lay out the options

for a potential I-A process or an RJ-SM process. Rae indicates they would be willing to go forward with an RJ-SM process.

The RJ-SM office reaches out to Von and Rae to complete pre-conferencing proceedings, including their own intake assessment rubric, sign consent to participate forms, iron out the logistics of when and where individual meetings will happen, determine each party's needs and hoped-for outcomes, and discuss possible models for arriving at a resolution. Von and Rae agree to participate in a facilitated dialogue using the conferencing model including support people; they also agree on the order in which they will speak. At the conference, they create an agreement that outlines that both students will go to counseling, Von will switch residence halls, and Rae will enroll in the university's mentoring program. The resolution agreement is reviewed and approved by the Title IX coordinator, signed by all parties, and the matter is closed. While the former couple decides to go their separate ways, they do so with a sense of closure, having exercised their voices and agency.

Chapter 7
RJ-SM Facilitation Best Practices

"We move at the speed of trust." And that can be delicate, and hard. And it can take a long time.[1]
— Mikayla W.-C. McCray

A restorative arts practitioner named Delight shares that relationships can follow several different scripts: power-over, power-within, and power-with. Power-over privileges majority identities through the marginalization of others. Power-within involves a person's sense of self-knowledge and worth emerging from the recognition and honoring of difference, and the capacity to imagine a hopeful future. Power-with is an earnest appreciation and combining of individual strengths to create a stronger collective. Delight emphasizes the importance of taking steps from power-over through power-within toward power-with, especially if the hope is equanimity, where all can feel empowered to use their voices and explore opportunities. Delight explains it this way:

If one moves directly from power-over to power-with, it can feel tokenizing, like "here is your seat at the table," when there is also the reality that the seat can be taken away. Or "here's the seat, but there will not be any changes to the norms or practices to make ownership of the seat feel true," acting as if being in that seat carries all the same weight for the recently added individual as it does for everyone else in the room.

Those of us who work in higher education are committed to safety, capacity building, and the activation of appropriate agency for students across the entire campus experience. For RJ-SM facilitators, this is all the more true. Power-over relationship dynamics cannot foster authentic independence, the intrinsic motivation necessary for the healthy development of self-determination, and the activation of personal and authentic agency. Ultimately, facilitators commit to "do no harm" through their RJ-SM work and, moreover, to empower individuals to learn to navigate challenges, be able to make informed decisions, and, in time, take ownership of their personal and academic growth, building the skills to be able to contribute meaningfully to the world. This chapter explores best practices in terms of facilitator qualities and skills and the training necessary to do RJ-SM work.

RJ-SM Facilitator Best Practices
A particular set of facilitation skills is necessary to do this work, including honoring individual agency, inviting reflective engagement, practicing

multi-partiality, understanding the impacts of sexual harm and trauma, discerning when disclosure or storytelling is not serving the process, and nurturing team- and self-care.

Honoring Individual Agency

Asking for help or information about institutional responses to misconduct can be an arduous first step for any student, faculty, or staff member, and their support people. By the time a case is referred to the RJ-SM office, a lot of institutional intervention has already happened, much of it without the input or even consent of the parties involved. The first best practice is centering the PH and honoring their agency and choice to the greatest extent possible, right out of the gate and throughout the process. This can be as simple as:

- Offering virtual or in-person meeting formats;
- Letting individuals know that they are welcome to, but do not have to, bring a support person with them;
- Having several seating options, and inviting individuals to sit wherever they are most comfortable;
- Asking before closing the office door, "Is it okay with you if we shut the door for our meeting, or would it be best to leave it open?" This helps affirm that the PH has choice and control over their privacy and bodily autonomy.

Inviting Reflective Engagement

A second important facilitation skill is the ability to ask relevant, open-ended questions, hold space, and respond reflectively. The most successful practitioners respect participant agency and move the process forward through an invitation to reflection so that the PH can assess their needs and the PCH can contemplate their obligations. This also means striking a balance between keeping timelines that a university Title IX office may have for an "adequate and timely response to known incidents of sexual harm," and the timetables, needs, and priorities of the individuals involved. Motivational Interviewing (MI) can be a valuable resource for learning how to do this. MI requires thoughtful listening and careful guidance to support the individual's personal, self-motivated, and self-directed evolutionary journey.[2] Learning to ask relevant, open-ended questions to inspire reflection and respond in open and empathic ways involves:

- Listening to spoken and unspoken messages;
- Verbally confirming the information shared in sincere, considerate, and constructive ways;
- Validating when appropriate;
- Offering relevant, open-hearted insights.

These skills are coupled with an ability to hold space by being present with people and offering empathetic support while maintaining one's own personal boundaries and self-awareness. Knowing when to lean in with questions and insight and when to hold space is a particular gift. While honoring the experiences, individual journeys, and personal growth of

all involved, facilitators must do their work to cultivate a sense of inner groundedness.

Practicing Multi-Partiality

Multi-partiality acknowledges that individual truths,
perspectives, needs, and nonnegotiables are valid
and may differ from others because individual perspectives are socially and experientially influenced,
and considers the influence of social identity and/or
social capital within communication.[3] It is especially
useful in discussions among individuals from diverse
social identity groups, as it aims to foster connections
across disparities.[4] Participants are invited to develop
a more complex understanding of how others experience and view situations and accept that we can have
different perspectives of the same situation without
invalidating individuals or their unique perspectives. The most successful facilitators embrace multi-
partiality and approach the work with a compassionate
but objective perspective that balances engagement,
courtesy, and regard for all parties while maintaining
emotional boundaries. This is no small feat.

Understanding the Impacts of Sexual Harm and Trauma

RJ-SM facilitators must appreciate the physical, emotional, psychological, and cognitive impacts of trauma
on individuals who have experienced sexual harm
and must hold space for the expressions of trauma
that show up. Specifically, they need to be clear that
a survivor's perceptions and recollections of experiences and the feelings related to the harm are valid,
regardless of what a Title IX policy defines as harm
or misconduct. Trauma impacts can make exact

recall challenging to sequence or put into words. While the story may not flow linearly, it does not mean the story is untrue. Taking the time to validate individuals, their decisions, and their feelings can make a substantial difference in survivorship and the ability to work through the RJ-SM process. Storytelling is important, as is creating space where the PH and their allies, and the PCH plus their support persons, can feel comfortable sharing their own stories in their own ways.

It is common for an individual who has experienced sexual harm to experience all kinds of emotional and physical responses to disclosure, including trembling, shaking, sweating, hot or cold flashes, and tears. It is critical that throughout the process, no party is pressured to disclose their story and that the facilitator recognizes when storytelling has become overwhelming. Individuals should feel supported in creating emotional boundaries to support their journey, or otherwise do what they need to maintain their well-being as much as possible.

Facilitators also need to be aware of and sensitive to the uncertainty and vigilance that PHs, particularly those of historically marginalized identities, may experience and project as they anticipate additional aggression or microaggression from the PCH, the facilitator, and/or because of the institution's processes (even the RJ-SM process). Given that "facts" are often hard to objectively identify in these harmful situations, many can struggle with questions like "Am I overreacting, being too sensitive, misinterpreting what just happened, or being paranoid?" This hypervigilance can lead to feelings of isolation, of not belonging, or that they cannot be successful in the current educational context. These experiences may result in the development of coping strategies that present as behavior changes, such as appearing overly friendly or exceptionally helpful, becoming more soft-spoken, or through marked passivity or ingratiating themselves to others to lessen the experiences and impacts of microaggressions and resulting alienation. If they can move beyond such negative impacts and the associated emotions, they might continue to struggle with feeling like they have in some way accepted the inappropriate behavior from others, resulting in a sense of guilt for not speaking up or otherwise resisting the aggression.

Discerning When Disclosure or Storytelling Is Not Serving the Process

Facilitators also need to exercise professional discernment in cases where disclosure and storytelling are not serving the process. While the impacts of trauma may factor into the intake and follow-up interactions, the purpose of storytelling in an RJ process is not primarily to surface painful emotions or relitigate the past. Rather, it is to eventually arrive at the place where the harms can be articulated, the needs can be named, and obligation(s) relative to the harm can be identified and addressed. If the process becomes too difficult, painful, or emotionally or physically unsafe for the parties to move through, it can become counterproductive. In that case, it may become necessary to pause, shift, or end the engagement. This takes a lot of wisdom, professional courage, and humility on the part of the facilitator. Should it become necessary, this is a great time to invite the perspective of the director or coordinator of the RJ-SM team or a peer

81

facilitator. RJ facilitators are not survivor advocates or counselors, so inviting the input of another who can offer some perspective on a particular situation is an important safety mechanism for all involved. Additional pre-conferencing work or other campus resources may need to be engaged during this pause, or it may be necessary to reroute the case to another campus process for resolution.

Nurturing Team- and Self-Care

Both community care and self-care are fundamental to building resiliency for this work. In the same way that harm does not happen in a vacuum, resilience and well-being are also shared. Professional coaching and regular supervision are fundamental to doing this work well. Take breaks, change out facilitators if needed, and take steps away from the work from time to time to maintain perspective on what is working and what is not working. It is also essential to build networks of support for facilitators. One way to do this is by holding regular circles for and with facilitators and anyone else in this work. If the team at a particular institution is small, reach out to colleagues at other institutions to build professional networks that extend the circle of care, accountability, problem-solving, celebration, and support beyond the individual institution.

Training Best Practices

Facilitator professional development begins with implicit-bias, anti-bias, and anti-racism training and skill building and continues with the integration and animation of these principles in the RJ-SM practices and operations.

We also suggest a collection of three trainings in dialogue processes. The first is general circle training, which lays the groundwork for ongoing practice. Of course circles can be offered for a variety of purposes—celebrations, community building, processing an issue, or honoring an individual or event, and also for preventative and responsive purposes at Tiers 0, 1, and 2. Harm circles, a Tier 2 practice specifically designed to address incidents that have already occurred, require additional specialized training. Finally, plan to receive training in facilitated dialogue between directly impacted parties and among groups (e.g., family group or community conferencing). Circle and conferencing processes are flexible models that can be adapted for large or small gatherings.

Teams interested in developing additional skills in the areas of trauma related to sexual harm could consider rape crisis counselor or domestic violence counselor training. Again, this is a unique skill set in addition to those of the restorative justice facilitator. While there is some overlap between the skills taught in RJ-SM practitioner training and crisis counselor or advocate training, they are distinct roles and services, and an RJ facilitator must maintain this distinction as they work in a particular RJ-SM case. If a case requires the services of a crisis counselor or survivor advocate, the case can be referred to those professionals before continuing or, in some cases, simultaneously with the RJ process.

It can be tempting to grasp new skills and feel prepared to apply them effectively. However, we recommend adequate time between each training course for learnings to percolate, practices to integrate, and for thoughtful evaluation before implementation. At the same time, a thorough understanding of various potential impacts, situational nuances, and outcomes often only emerges through repeated practice. Even with training, understanding, and adequate time, we recommend a period of apprenticeship with a seasoned practitioner, followed by joint practice between two trained facilitators.

A Case in Point: Lee and Morgan

Lee, a graduate student from China, has been accused of sexual harassment by a fellow graduate student, Morgan, who is from the US. Morgan reports inappropriate comments and incidents of unwelcome advances, amounting to a hostile environment created by Lee, to the Title IX office. These issues have occurred within the research team environment, which includes other graduate students and supervising faculty researchers. Upon receiving Morgan's complaint, the case is referred to a trained RJ-SM facilitator. In pre-conferencing meetings with Morgan, it becomes apparent that the issues are broader, and that other students are causing and experiencing harm beyond Lee and Morgan. In pre-conferencing with Lee, the facilitator learns that one of the issues is different understandings of gender roles based on cultural background.

Morgan is willing to use shuttle negotiation to reach an arrangement where research can continue as smoothly as possible given what has happened. As shuttle negotiations progress, Morgan requests a circle process with Lee and the other graduate students on the research team to discuss the broader issues and their impacts as part of the final resolution agreement. They also request that the faculty members be made aware of the specifics of the resolution agreement that would impact research team interactions in the lab moving forward. To maintain agency and honor the privacy of both Morgan and Lee, the facilitator is mindful to clarify what Morgan and Lee would like shared with the faculty and other graduate students, and how they would like it shared. The faculty members are grateful to be included and commit to honoring their responsibilities to help cultivate a team culture that is more resistant to harassment by implementing specific suggestions made by Morgan and the other graduate students. All parties agree to these outcomes. The RJ-SM team carefully facilitates the circle process using the following questions:

- What personal values do you bring to the team that can help it operate optimally?
- How does your team create a positive (inclusive/supportive/respectful) climate?
- How does your team struggle to create a positive (inclusive/supportive/respectful) climate?
- What next steps would you like to see to improve the team climate and address your concerns?
- What are your takeaways from this circle process?

As a result of the circle process, the students gain a more nuanced understanding of their colleagues' personal and cultural backgrounds, values, and educational priorities. They also develop a set of specific suggestions to present to the faculty for implementation moving forward: (1) initiate a simple but carefully structured onboarding process for each new team member to share team values, expectations, and norms, as well as campus and community policies and resources for support and well-being; and (2) implement a practice of regularly checking in with students, initially to establish personal and professional goals, and then to discuss organizational climate and safety ongoing. The RJ-SM team ensures the implementation of the agreement developed between Lee and Morgan, provides ongoing support as needed, and establishes a follow-up schedule to assess progress with the faculty and student team, address emerging issues, and ensure that all parties are satisfied with the outcomes.

Chapter 8
Campus Climate and Culture

The things we fear most in organizations—fluctuations, disturbances, imbalances—need not be signs of an impending disorder that will destroy us. Instead, fluctuations are the primary source of creativity. [1]

—Dr. Margaret J. Wheatley

The impact that institutional climate and culture play in successfully implementing any response to relationship violence or sexual misconduct (RVSM), be it a whole school approach or a Tier 2 RJ-SM process, cannot be minimized or underestimated. Predictably, there will be tangible "climate and culture issues," whose absence or presence affects the viability of a restorative justice policy and procedural additives.

If the institution were compared to a tree found in a forest, climate would amount to rain, wind, and sun. These are larger, external, but variable realities over which an institution has no control, but which

87

impact its operations, growth, and development, like politics and even pandemics. A healthy, well-established institution will weather climate challenges like a thriving tree: it may bend in the wind but not succumb to it. Cultural factors are the local elements over which the institution has more control. Like a tree's soil quality and root depth, which are essential to a tree's ability to weather the storm, grow, and develop, these factors change more slowly and over more extended periods.

Ultimately, a healthy institutional climate and culture foster inclusivity, diversity, and a more viable approach to restorative justice initiatives. This chapter introduces our own experiences, via the Case in Point, and the lessons about climate and culture that emerge from it. We explore the cultural and climate factors that influenced this project using the steps outlined in chapter 5 to offer a view of how culture and climate can influence every stage of the development process. The chapter closes with a discussion of how cultural and climate shifts not only help with the development of an RJ-SM program but also work to build more socially just campus communities.

A Case in Point: Culture and Climate Challenges to Program Design and Implementation

As the Title IX coordinator and the assistant director of Student Accountability and Restorative Justice, we were charged with designing an RJ-SM Title IX policy additive. However, the full development of an RJ-SM program did not come to fruition during our tenure because of old organizational wounds, newer institutional traumas, and limitations that needed to be addressed before a project like this could have been fully realized.

Examine and Assess

Our journey toward implementation began with work on a university-wide committee tasked with assessing institutional policies for their effectiveness in meeting the needs of harmed parties. The task force included administrative representatives, student affairs staff, faculty, and student representatives. During the committee's work, changes in Title IX legislation were forecasted that would allow for the inclusion of RJ for formal resolutions in cases of alleged campus sexual misconduct. The committee was intrigued—did the possibility exist to develop additional procedures to enhance the existing Title IX responses to better address the harms and needs resulting from these incidents? Fueled by our curiosity and optimism, and with the endorsement of university leadership, we designed a participatory action research-styled project to explore why and how the university's existing sexual and gender-based misconduct policy and procedure were failing to meet the needs of individuals affected by RVSM within the campus community and assess the possible benefits of offering an additional RJ-informed, institutionally facilitated procedure.

In preparing for a future implementation of the policy proposal, the committee took a two-pronged approach. First, they established the alignment between the institution's core values of community and peace-building and RJ's fundamental principles. This alignment indicated that RJ-SM could theoretically be a good fit for the university. Then, the current Title IX policy was assessed to find those places where it could be made more attentive to the needs of various stakeholders and generally carried out in as restorative a way as possible. In doing this policy review, the committee was also able to identify those places where the policy would need amendment if we were to provide a procedural additive.

Staff and Invest

Unfortunately, this project was initiated during significant organizational volatility and unpredictability. Many small to mid-sized universities across the US struggled with decreasing prospective student pools and an increase of students who faced difficulties with college preparedness, staying enrolled, and eventually graduating.[2] As a result, university administrative services went above and beyond to attract and retain students. At the same time, faculty and staff worked harder than ever, constantly adapting their approaches and offerings to meet emerging student needs. University leadership looked for entrepreneurial strategies that provided as high a return on investment as possible and found creative ways to save resources, including staffing and programmatic changes, to seize opportunities and minimize risks to the institution. Most, if not all, departments were understaffed and overwhelmed. These local issues led to an extended sense of instability within the university and took hold within the culture. Over time, new leaders who brought energy, perspective, and vision were hired, leading to a more stable and positive environment. Unfortunately, just as things seemed to be settling down, the COVID-19 pandemic struck, causing upheaval across the globe, including within higher education.

Design and Detail

Despite the hurdles, months were dedicated to designing and carefully detailing every aspect of the Title IX RJ-SM policy additive. As mentioned, the process saw some wins and losses. For example, when general counsel was asked to weigh in, they gave theoretical approval for the draft policy. With that assurance, procedures were developed and tested with various community stakeholder groups for input and feedback. These conversations were critical in improving and fine-tuning the RJ-SM proposal to fit the needs of the specific community for which it was being designed.

Collaborate and Communicate

The university-wide committee tasked with assessing institutional policies, student affairs, and Title IX offices, along with several key university influence leaders and administrators including the chief academic officer and the vice president of inclusive excellence were significant stakeholders and communicators. In gathering stakeholder input, broader issues were communicated in the policy design and detail process. First, several individuals noted that before a specific RJ-informed procedural additive could be developed, there was a need to grapple with accountability at the institutional level. For example, one stakeholder asked, "Shouldn't we address broader systemic issues as well?" while another community member said, "I'm still worried about our campus and community culture—how can we raise awareness about the widespread need for this and also develop prevention options?" Stakeholders highlighted that, beyond just a remedies-based, complainant-driven process focusing on specific incidents (a Tier 2 response), there might be a need for more extensive institutional cultural shifts concerning issues related to sex and power (Tiers 0 and 1).

Another leading issue that the design and detailing conversations revealed was a fundamental lack of trust in the institution. Many students, faculty, and staff believed that institutional processes could not be trusted, so there was skepticism that this new procedure would be any different. Much of this was attributed to the institutional turbulence that had resulted in layoffs, reductions, and program closures, which exacerbated a sense of instability and vulnerability for many.

Implement and Evaluate

While climate factors may be outside of institutional control, cultural dynamics can be challenged, navigated, and leveraged for increased and ongoing campus vitality. For example, when layoffs and cutbacks resulted in general malaise, the administration could have shown support for innovation and creativity and set cultural expectations for collaborative teamwork toward shared goals. As this was not happening, endorsement for this initiative was seen as insincere and resulted in brittle campus support. This aligns with what Karp and Williamsen have said, that "although support for restorative justice—including in matters of sexual harm—is growing, many people mistrust that institutions will implement restorative justice with fidelity and in good faith."[3]

Trust-building and addressing institutional betrayal on a proactive and ongoing basis are necessary for the development and effective use of RJ-SM. In this specific case, the campus community expressed general trust in the individuals in charge of campus accountability processes but a lack of trust in the institution and its established or existing structures and procedures.

When the climate is challenging and the culture lacks vitality, an RJ-SM initiative either will not be able to launch or will result in the development of a novel gimmick that lacks the integrity to advance from implementation through the achievement of the longer-term goals to offer a fresh approach to healing, personal growth, and accountability.[4] Ultimately, while there was initial support for the project from the institution, there was a lack of agreement among essential decision-makers within the institution regarding implementing an RJ-SM facilitated process.

Lessons Learned from Climate and Culture

We learned a lot from the implementation experience, lessons that illustrate issues and dynamics relevant to a variety of educational institutions across differing contexts. First was the discovery that an institution's ability to prioritize a project like this depends on various factors related to the campus environment and general institutional well-being. It is essential to recognize that a project focused on improving the minimum requirements set by the federal government is assessed and considered within the context of a broader conversation and plan regarding the overall atmosphere and values on campus. This is why we are particularly supportive of the whole-campus approach, with its focus on institutional vitality and holistic community well-being. This work begins with education, training, and skill-set cultivation among individual leaders and consultation with administration, faculty, and staff leaders across Tiers 0, 1, and 2. These integrated efforts can go a long way to support the development of campus climates that are resistant to sexual and gender-based harassment.[5]

Any higher education institution working within a challenging climate and culture and attempting to advance equity and justice generally, or through specific initiatives such as an RJ-SM program, needs straightforward and sincere support and endorsement from university administrators, key decision-makers, and stakeholders. When trust is lacking, institutions can demonstrate a desire to build it back by (1) clear communication as to how policy might apply in these sorts of [hypothetical] situations and how processes typically unfold, (2) being as transparent as possible about the harms that have been experienced, and (3) identifying any individual responsibility for those harms and/or collective/institutional failures (at least to the generalized extent possible in each situation).[6]

Most higher education institutions have faced significant challenges in recent years, including mental and physical health challenges, staffing cuts or high turnover, and resource limitations. While it may be exciting to discover the promise of RJ-SM and have a well-thought-out plan to develop such a program, as we have seen, excitement does not guarantee that the plan will be implemented and achieve the desired results.[7] Even though the implementation did not happen as expected, it is worth remembering that sometimes disorder or challenges can be the starting point for important changes, as Margaret Wheatley suggests in the quote that opens this chapter.

Start Slow and Be Creative

We are still committed to the belief that while meeting Title IX requirements, it is equally important to go beyond minimum standards to address the harms and needs experienced by the PH and others impacted by RVSM in ways that support capacity, facilitate agency, and repair harm in whatever ways are possible. For us, this connects our work to the bigger movement toward increasing equity and justice within our institutions and beyond. It is through meeting the needs of the most vulnerable that just educational communities are created.[8] The successful implementation of an RJ-SM program emerges from, and will certainly result in, significant cultural shifts toward justice, where compassion, care, repair, and accountability are known more broadly within our institutions. Shifting our organizational cultures toward greater wholeness and well-being not only improves the possibilities for successful implementation of programs like RJ-SM that advance social justice, but also indicates support for the cultivation of educational communities that care more generally about equity, justice, belonging, well-being, and sustainability. This promise gives us hope and energy for the work ahead.

Chapter 9
The Promise of RJ for Sexual Harms in Campus Contexts

What is the quality of your intent?[1]
—Supreme Court Justice Thurgood Marshall

Working in the Title IX space or a student conduct office handling any kind of relationship violence, sexual misconduct, or harm repair can be grueling. The process of implementing restorative justice policies and practices to respond to campus-based sexual harm is also not easy! While the path ahead may seem daunting, the potential rewards are worth it. Use the implementation journey as a community-building exercise with like-minded campus stakeholders, and be reassured that once implemented, RJ extends the possibility of a more positive and sustainable working and learning environment for all. When short-term challenges arise, keep the long-term vision in sight with these final ideas: protect the "magic real estate"; be creative and dream; feel, don't just think; and stray from the beaten path.

Protect the "Magic Real Estate"

Once you have an RJ-SM program, protect the "magic real estate," that "space between an incident and the selected resolution pathway. Often, it is in this space that the greatest potential exists for the use of educational, effective, creative, flexible, restorative, and socially just resolution methods."[2] The magic real estate invites partnerships, creativity, and innovation that might have otherwise been inaccessible or impossible. Remaining on the proscribed course (ways of doing things that have been "off limits") and prescribed pathways (the "official" ways of doing things) leads to immobilization, arrested curiosity and learning, and stunted growth. Lean into the intricacies and iterative nature of restorative justice. Holding this kind of space throughout both the program development and implementation phases, and even individual facilitated processes, creates the necessary room for restorative justice to move "at the speed of trust," with the flexibility to accommodate the needs that arise, as well as making room for obligations to be met.

Be Creative and Dream

Our journey was challenging, inviting creativity at each next step. That led us to this project. When you reach a seeming dead end, pause, regroup, and then embrace a creativity that looks at the needs of those who stand to gain the most, engaging their questions. That could be:

- Title IX personnel who may be frustrated and exhausted by business as usual;
- Student government officers who want to bring something fresh and exciting to campus;

98

- Student affairs professionals who are ready
  to think outside the box;
- PHs and PCHs who have been dissatisfied
  with their own experiences and want others
  to have different kinds of experiences;
- Members of general counsel who are curious
  about resolution options that divert cases
  from a litigious response;
- Faculty who are interested in RJ on an
  intellectual level or as a matter of principle.

Invite fresh conversations with these individuals to explore ways to move forward collectively. In this case, it is worth knowing and reminding stakeholders that restorative justice may require investment and infrastructure on the front end but will gain potential efficiencies in the long term, through higher rates of participant satisfaction and increased feelings of institutional affinity for various stakeholder groups. Keep working at it; dream and strive for what has value.

Feel, Don't Just Think

We recommend that those who are taking the project-lead role explore their personal "why" for embarking on this journey and be transparent about what they hope will come of it. We had conversations around these questions in the run-up to our shared process, naming our mutual commitment to integrity in Title IX compliance *and* a deep desire to see that Title IX processes are carried out in compassionate and caring ways that pay attention to human needs. We aim to be thoughtful about these issues, grounded in the best research. As restorative justice practitioners, we also strive to bring heart to the issues. In academia, it is easy to intellectualize a thing to death, asking: "What about this detail, principle, or model?" "What is the justification or evidence to show this is true?" Many in higher education are too quick to dismiss things without scientific labels and "academically valid" processes or data. However, using restorative values as building blocks, the ability to navigate the "what ifs" in authentic and universally beneficial ways feels possible. In fact, we encourage *feeling* through projects with as much energy as *thinking* through them, as Dr. Fania Davis aptly elaborates on the words of the Rev. Dr. Martin Luther King Jr.: "Justice is love correcting that which revolts against love."

Stray from the Beaten Path

An aspect of restorative justice that is as difficult as it is exciting is the need to continue straying from the beaten path and avoiding the temptation to acquiesce to the status quo. You read that right: continue to stray from the beaten path. As our restorative justice journeys advance, we resist the urge to have our actions mirror the systems we have grown up in and been accustomed to. However, we do not need new versions of the same systems! Keeping our minds and hearts open to the next right step means leaning into that magic real estate and trusting the restorative values, questions, building blocks, and hallmarks as our scaffolding. "Blue sky thinking" becomes our guiding principle; instead of asking "What do we have to do?" we ask ourselves "What do we get to do?"

A Case in Point: Frankie and August, Part 2

We met Frankie and August at the end of chapter 2. You'll recall that first-year student Frankie engages in unwelcome conduct and nonconsensual interactions with student leader August, who has decided to talk to the Title IX office about her concerns. As the Title IX office is working through its process to address the complaint, life on campus becomes miserable for August, Frankie, and even their broader communities. August returns to the Title IX office to ask if there is another way to deal with the situation because she feels on edge, distracted, and disengaged. The Title IX office suggests the possibility of a referral to the RJ-SM team. August is intrigued to learn more. Eventually, August and Frankie indicate their openness to an RJ-SM process and agree to a circle process through pre-conferencing and some shuttle negotiation.

August invites a trusted university staff member to accompany her. Frankie asks the director of student disability services, a close mentor to him, to join in support. Throughout the conversation, August can identify feelings of discomfort, worry, and fear because of Frankie's behavior, and anger about how the situation has developed. Frankie is surprised to learn these things from August and shares that one of the realities of his life as a person with autism is that he has a more challenging time than others in reading social cues. When August explains the impact of his behavior, Frankie is very remorseful and wants to know what he can do to make it up to her. With the facilitator's guidance and the involvement of their support people, August and Frankie develop a written agreement outlining specific actions and commitments to address the harm caused and prevent future incidents. The agreement is not punitive but aims to promote safety, learning, and growth. August is interested in interning with the office of student disabilities services, so this is written into the resolution agreement. Frankie will participate in structured one-on-one coaching sessions to support his emerging awareness of consent and boundaries and general psychosocial development. This coaching will be provided through the office of the dean of students. In a post-process evaluation, August says, "Before this, I felt stuck. However, through this process, I feel more at peace on campus and generally more confident. This was a good experience, and even though it wasn't easy, I'm glad I did it." Frankie says, "It opened my eyes to how my actions affected someone else. I'm glad I could learn from the experience."

When we consider RJ fundamentals, the next right step becomes clear and easy to understand. Think about who has been affected, what they need, and whose job it is to help them. Be imaginative in finding answers to these questions. Ultimately, the fundamentals can be applied to both straightforward and complex issues, whether they involve larger institutions, cultural aspects, environmental changes, or individual experiences of harm. As Dr. Cornel West says, "Justice is what love looks like in public."[3] This is an invitation and a reminder of the perspective we must keep at the heart of this work:

- What is the next right step?
- What is essential?
- What does love look like?

Resources for Further Learning

"Five Things Student Affairs Administrators Should Know About Restorative Justice and Campus Sexual Harm," Policy brief by David Karp and Kaaren Williamsen, National Association of Student Personnel Administrators, https://www.naspa.org /report/five-things-student-affairs-administrators -should-know-about-restorative-justice-and-campus -sexual-harm

Applying Restorative Justice to Campus Sexual Misconduct: A Guide to Emerging Practices, edited by Kaaren Williamsen and Erik Wessel (London: Routledge, 2023)

"Restorative Justice Implementation Guide: A Whole School Approach," Oakland Unified School District, https://www.ousd.org/restorative-justice/resources

"12 Indicators of Restorative Practices Implementation: Checklists for Administrators," Rutgers University, https://www.naesp.org/wp-content/uploads/2021 /01/12_Indicators_of_RP_Implementation _Checklists_FINAL.original.1560275926-2.pdf

"2022 Rubric on Areas of Work for Preventing Sexual Harassment in Higher Education," National Academies of Sciences, Engineering, and Medicine, https:

//nap.nationalacademies.org/resource/26741/2022
_Rubric_on_Areas_of_Work_for_Preventing
_Sexual_Harassment_in_Higher_Education.pdf
"Addressing Sexual and Relationship Violence: A
Trauma-Informed Approach," American College
Health Association, https://www.acha.org/ACHA
/Resources/Addressing_Sexual_and_Relationship
_Violence_A_Trauma_Informed_Approach.aspx
"Sexual Citizens Toolkit," Jennifer S. Hirsch and Shamus
Khan, https://www.sexualcitizens.com/space-toolkit
"Creative Interventions Toolkit: A Practical Guide to
Stop Interpersonal Violence," https://www.creative
-interventions.org/toolkit/

Training Resources
The Ahimsa Collective—https://www.ahimsacol
lective.net/what-we-do
**University of San Diego Center for Restorative
Justice** (see link to RJ training for Campus Sexual Harm, Title IX)—https://www.sandiego.edu/soles
/centers-and-institutes/restorative-justice/

Endnotes

Chapter 1

1 James Baldwin, "As Much Truth As One Can Bear," *The New York Times,* January 14, 1962, 11.

2 Fania Davis, *The Little Book of Race and Restorative Justice: Black Lives, Healing, and US Social Transformation* (New York: Skyhorse Publishing, 2019).

3 Mary Koss, Jay Wilgus, and Kaaren Williamsen, "Campus Sexual Misconduct: Restorative Justice Approaches to Enhance Compliance With Title IX Guidance," *Trauma, Violence & Abuse* 15, no. 3 (2014): 242-57, https://www.jstor.org/stable /26876513.

4 David Cantor et al., *Report on the AAU Climate Survey on Sexual Assault and Sexual Misconduct,* Washington, DC: Association of American Universities, 2019.

5 Mindy Bergman, et al., "The (un) reasonableness of reporting: Antecedents and consequences of reporting sexual harassment," *Journal of Applied Psychology* 87 (2002): 230.

6 Howard Zehr. *The Little Book of Restorative Justice* (New York: Skyhorse Publishing, 2015).

7   Theo Gavrielides, ed. *Routledge International Handbook of Restorative Justice*, 1st ed. (London: Routledge, 2018), https://doi.org/10.4324/97813 15613512.

8   Katherine Beaty Chiste, "Origins of Modern Restorative Justice: Five Examples from the English-Speaking World," *UBC Law Review*, 33 (2013): 46, https://canlii.ca/t/7n6l6; Paora Moyle and Juan Tauri, "Māori, Family Group Conferencing and the Mystifications of Restorative Justice," *Victims & Offenders*, 11, no. 1-20 (2016): 87–106; Zehr, *The Little Book of Restorative Justice*.

9   Patricia Cook-Craig et al., "Challenge and opportunity in evaluating a diffusion-based active bystanding prevention program: Green Dot in high schools," *Violence Against Women* vol. 20, 10 (2014): 1179–202, doi:10.1177/1077801214551288.

10 Zora Neale Hurston, *Their Eyes Were Watching God* (New York: Harper Perennial Modern Classics, 2006), 21.

Chapter 2

1   James Keenan, *Virtues for Ordinary Christians* (Kansas City: Sheed & Ward, 1996), 69.

2   Kimberlé Williams Crenshaw, "Intersectionality, Identity Politics, and Violence Against Women of Color" in *The Public Nature of Private Violence*, edited by Martha Albertson Fineman and Roxanne Mykitiuk (London: Routledge, 1994), 93–118, https://doi.org/10.4324/9780203060902.

3   Title IX of the Education Amendments Act of 1972, 20 U.S.C. §§1681–1688 (2018, 2020).

4   Deondra Rose, "Regulating Opportunity: Title IX and the Birth of Gender-Conscious Higher Education Policy," *Journal of Policy History* 27,

no. 1 (2015): 157–183, doi:https://doi.org/10.1017
/S0898030614000396.

5   Amy Cyphert, "The Devil Is in the Details:
    Exploring Restorative Justice As an Option for
    Campus Sexual Assault Responses Under Title IX
    (2018)," *Denver Law Review* 96, no. 1 (2018): 69.

6   Zehr, *The Little Book of Restorative Justice: Revised
    & Updated.* (New York: Good Books, 2015).

7   Charles Barton, *Restorative Justice: The Empowerment
    Model* (Sydney: Hawkins Press, 2003).

8   David R. Karp and Casey Sacks, "Student Conduct,
    Restorative Justice, and Student Development:
    Findings from the STARR Project: A Student
    Accountability and Restorative Research Project,"
    Contemporary Justice Review 17, no. 2 (2014):
    154–172, doi:https://doi.org/10.1080/10282580.20
    14.915140.

9   Patricia M. King, "Principles of Development
    and Developmental Change Underlying Theories
    of Cognitive and Moral Development," *Journal
    of College Student Development* 50, no. 6 (2009):
    597–620, doi:https://doi.org/10.1353/csd.0.0104;
    Jennifer Meyer Schrage and Nancy Geist
    Giacomini, eds, *Reframing Campus Conflict: Student
    Conduct Practice Through the Lens of Inclusive
    Excellence*, 2nd ed. (New York: Routledge, 2020),
    https://doi.org/10.4324/9781003446736.

10 Barton, *Restorative Justice: The Empowerment
    Model*; Cyphert, "The Devil Is in the Details."

11 Kathryn J. Holland and Lilia M. Cortina, "'It
    Happens to Girls all the Time': Examining Sexual
    Assault Survivors' Reasons for Not Using Campus
    Supports," *American Journal of Community
    Psychology* 59, no. 1 (2017): 50–64, doi:https://doi
    .org/10.1002/ajcp.12126.

12 Carly Parnitzke Smith and Jennifer J. Freyd, "Institutional Betrayal," *The American Psychologist* 69, no. 6 (2014): 575–587, https://doi.org/10.1037/a0037564.

13 Cyphert, "The Devil Is in the Details"; Shamus R. Khan et al., "'I Didn't Want to Be "That Girl"': The Social Risks of Labeling, Telling, and Reporting Sexual Assault," *Sociological Science* 5, no. 7 (2018): 432–460, doi:https://doi.org/10.15195/v5.a19; Koss, Wilgus, Williamsen, "Campus Sexual Misconduct: Restorative Justice Approaches to Enhance Compliance With Title IX Guidance"; Clare McGlynn and Nicole Westmarland, "Kaleidoscopic Justice: Sexual Violence and Victim-Survivors' Perceptions of Justice," *Social & Legal Studies* 28, no. 2 (2019): 179–201, doi:https://doi.org/10.1177/0964663918761200; Clare McGlynn, Nicole Westmarland, and Nikki Godden, "'I Just Wanted Him to Hear Me': Sexual Violence and the Possibilities of Restorative Justice," *Journal of Law and Society* 39, no. 2 (2012): 213–240, doi:https://doi.org/10.1111/j.1467-6478.2012.00579.x.; Larke Huang et al., *SAMHSA's Concept of Trauma and Guidance for a Trauma-Informed Approach* (Rockville, MD: U.S. Department of Health & Human Services: Substance Abuse and Mental Health Services Administration), HHS Publication No. (SMA) 14-4884, 2014.

14 Kim Webb and Mary Wyandt-Hiebert, et al., *Addressing Sexual And Relationship Violence: A Trauma-Informed Approach* (Silver Spring, MD: American College Health Association, 2018); Shannon Harper, Jon Maskaly, Anne Kirkner, and Katherine Lorenz, "Enhancing Title IX Due Process Standards in Campus Sexual Assault Adjudication:

Considering the Roles of Distributive, Procedural, and Restorative Justice," *Journal of School Violence* 16, no. 3 (2017): 302–316, doi:https://doi.org/10.1 080/15388220.2017.1318578.

15 There are some specific dynamics to consider in working restoratively with people who are autistic or otherwise neurodivergent. In some cases, restorative practices, and specifically RJ-SM, are not appropriate, and in other campus-based cases it is precisely the correct type of intervention to meet the learning and socialization needs of the individuals involved. We recommend reading Nicholas Burnett and Margaret Thorsborne's *Restorative Practice and Special Needs* to learn more.

Chapter 3

1   Dr. Martin Luther King Jr., "Remaining Awake Through a Great Revolution," Speech given at the National Cathedral, March 31, 1968.

2   Zehr, *The Little Book of Restorative Justice*; Madison Orcutt, Patricia Petrowski, David Karp, Jordan Draper, "Restorative Justice Approaches to the Informal Resolution of Student Sexual Misconduct," *Journal of College and University Law* 45, no. 2 (2020): 1–76.

3   Orcutt, Petrowski, Karp, and Draper, "Restorative Justice Approaches."

4   Brunilda Pali, "Aligning Action Research And Restorative Justice: Highlighting Epistemological Tensions," *Journal of Extreme Anthropology* 3, no. 1 (2019): 7–29, https://doi.org/10.5617/jea.6688; Rosalie Young. "Images of Restorative Justice Theory," edited by Robert Mackay, Marko Bošnjak, Johan Deklerck, Christa Pelikan, Bas van Stokkom,

and Martin Wright, *Law & Society Review*, 43, no. 2 (2009), 447–449, doi:10.1111/j.1540-5893.2009.00378_5.x.

5   Zehr, *The Little Book of Restorative Justice.*

CHAPTER 4

1   Margaret J. Wheatley, *Finding our Way: Leadership for an Uncertain Time* (Oakland, CA: Berrett-Koehler Publishers, 2005): 262.

2   David Karp and Kaaren Williamsen, "Five Things Student Affairs Administrators Should Know About Restorative Justice and Campus Sexual Harm" [Policy Brief] (Washington, DC: NASPA, Student Affairs Administrators in Higher Education, 2020).

3   Carolyn Boyes-Watson and Kay Pranis, *Circle Forward: Building a Restorative School Community* (St. Paul, MN: Living Justice Press, 2020): 69.

4   Kelly Maxwell, Biren Ratnesh Nagda, and Monita Thompson, *Facilitating Intergroup Dialogues: Bridging Differences, Catalyzing Change* (New York: Routledge, 2011), doi:10.4324/9781003444756; Ximena Zúñiga, Biren Nagda, Mark Chesler, and Adena Cytron-Walker, "Intergroup Dialogue In Higher Education: Meaningful Learning About Social Justice," *ASHE Higher Education Report Series*, 32, no. 4 (2007): 1–128.

5   Boyes-Watson and Pranis, *Circle Forward*; see also David Yusem et al., "Restorative Justice Implementation Guide: A Whole School Approach."

6   Dorothy Vaandering and Kathy Evans, *The Little Book of Restorative Justice in Education: Fostering Responsibility, Healing, and Hope in Schools* (New York: Skyhorse Publishing, 2016); Davis, *The Little Book of Race and Restorative Justice.*

7 Joan Tabachnick and Jay Wilgus, "Specialized Interventions for Addressing Problematic Sexual Behavior" in *Applying Restorative Justice to Campus Sexual Misconduct: A Guide to Emerging Practices*, edited by Kaaren Williamsen, and Erik Wessel (New York: Routledge, 2023): 97–114.

8 Martin Clarke, Susan Brown, and Birgit Völlm, "Circles of Support and Accountability for Sex Offenders: A Systematic Review of Outcomes," *Sexual Abuse* 29, no. 5 (Los Angeles: SAGE Publications, 2017).

9 Koss, Wilgus, Williamsen, "Campus Sexual Misconduct: Restorative Justice Approaches to Enhance Compliance with Title IX Guidance."

10 The Science-based Treatment, Accountability, and Risk Reduction for Sexual Assault (STARRSA) Active Psychoeducation (AP), University of Michigan, Office of Student Conflict Resolution: https://oscr.umich.edu/starrsa.

11 See Shana Hormann and Pat Vivian's Strengths and Shadows Model (2013) at http://organizationaltraumaandhealing.com/resources.

Chapter 5

1 Angela Davis, nd. (As with many other important sayings given to us by significant African American thought leaders, this quote has been widely attributed to Angela Davis, but is not definitively able to be quoted. This is common in oral traditions.)

Chapter 6

1 Margaret J. Wheatley, *Turning To One Another: Simple Conversations To Restore Hope To Restore*

Hope To The Future (Oakland, CA: Berrett-Koehler Publishers, 2009): 55.

2 Courtney Stevens, Cindy Liu, and Justin Chen, "Racial/Ethnic Disparities in U.S. College Students' Experience: Discrimination as an Impediment to Academic Performance," *Journal of American College Health*, 66, no. 7 (2018): 665–673, doi:10.1 080/07448481.2018.1452745.

3 University of California. *SMART Goals: A How to Guide*, 2016–17; https://med.stanford.edu/content/dam/sm/s-spire/documents/How-to-write-SMART-Goals-v2.pdf.

4 These characteristics also distinguish RJ from the practice of mediation. Unlike RJ, mediation does not necessitate one party acknowledging their responsibility for harm, does not explicitly account for various power dynamics between the parties, does not require extensive pre-conferencing preparation between the facilitator and the parties involved, and does not consider community or institutional factors that may have a stake of some kind in the resolution. For more, see David Karp, Julie Shackford-Bradley, Robin Wilson, and Kaaren Williamsen, "Campus PRISM: A Report on Promoting Restorative Initiatives For Sexual Misconduct On College Campuses," *School of Leadership and Education Sciences: Faculty Scholarship*, 2016: 36, https://digital.sandiego.edu/soles-faculty/36.

Chapter 7
1 Mikayla W.-C. McCray, quoting and elaborating on Stephen Covey, *The Speed of Trust* (London: Simon & Schuster, 2008).

2   William Miller and Stephen Rollnick, *Motivational Interviewing: Helping People Change*, 4th ed. (New York: Guilford Press, 2023).

3   Robbie Routenberg, Elizabeth Thompson, and Rhian Waterberg, *When Neutrality Is Not Enough: Wrestling With the Challenges of Multipartiality* (New York: Routledge, 2013), doi:10.4324/9781003447580-13.

4   Ibid.

Chapter 8

1   Margaret J. Wheatley, *Leadership and the New Science: Learning about Organization from an Orderly Universe* (Oakland, CA: Berrett-Koehler Publishers, 1992): 19.

2   Anemona Hartocollis, "Colleges Running Low on Money Worry Students Will Vanish, Too: Foreign Desk," *The New York Times*, April 16, 2020; Mitch Smith. "At Struggling Rural Colleges, No Future for History Degrees," *The New York Times*, January 13, 2019; Sam Stall, "A Different Kind of Challenge," *Indianapolis Business Journal*, (Indianapolis: IBJ Corporation, 2018): 17A–18A.

3   David Karp and Kaaren Williamsen, "Five Things Student Affairs Administrators Should Know About Restorative Justice and Campus Sexual Harm" [Policy Brief] (Washington, DC: NASPA, Student Affairs Administrators in Higher Education, 2020): 12.

4   Belinda Hopkins, "From Restorative Justice to Restorative Culture," *Revista de Asistenţă Socială* 4, no. 4 (2015).

5   Rachel Roth Sawatzky, "Implementation of Institutionally Facilitated Restorative Justice

Approaches to Address Campus Sexual Harm" in *Applying Restorative Justice to Campus Sexual Misconduct: A Guide to Emerging Practices*, edited by Kaaren Williamsen and Erik Wessel (New York: Routledge, 2023), 196–208.

6 Ibid.

7 Mostafa Safdari Ranjbar, Mohsen Akbarpour Shirazi, and Mojtaba Blooki, "Interaction Among Intra-Organizational Factors Effective in Successful Strategy Execution: An Analytical View," *Journal of Strategy and Management*, 7, no. 2 (2014): 127–154.

Clayton Smith, Janet Hyde, Tina Falkner, and Christine Kerlin, "The Role of Organizational Change Management in Successful Strategic Enrollment Management Implementation," *Strategic Enrollment Management Quarterly*, 8, no. 2 (2020): 31–40.

8 Judah Oudshoorn, Lorraine Stutzman Amstutz, and Michelle Jackett, *The Little Book of Restorative Justice for Sexual Abuse: Hope through Trauma* (New York: Skyhorse Publishing, 2015).

Chapter 9

1 Thurgood Marshall, *Brown v. Board of Education of Topeka*, U.S. Supreme Court, May 17, 1954.

2 Jennifer Meyer Schrage and Nancy Geist Giacomini, eds, *Reframing Campus Conflict: Student Conduct Practice Through the Lens of Inclusive Excellence*, 2nd ed. (New York: Routledge, 2020): 66.

3 Cornel West, "Justice is What Love Looks Like in Public," speech, Howard University, April 2011, https://www.youtube.com/watch?v=nGqP7S_WO6o&t=21s.

Published titles include:

The Little Book of Restorative Justice: Revised & Updated,
by Howard Zehr
The Little Book of Conflict Transformation, by John Paul Lederach
The Little Book of Family Group Conferences, New-Zealand Style,
by Allan MacRae and Howard Zehr
The Little Book of Strategic Peacebuilding, by Lisa Schirch
The Little Book of Strategic Negotiation,
by Jayne Seminare Docherty
The Little Book of Circle Processes, by Kay Pranis
The Little Book of Contemplative Photography, by Howard Zehr
The Little Book of Restorative Discipline for Schools, by Lorraine Stutzman
Amstutz and Judy H. Mullet
The Little Book of Trauma Healing, by Carolyn Yoder
The Little Book of Biblical Justice, by Chris Marshall
The Little Book of Restorative Justice for People in Prison,
by Barb Toews
The Little Book of Cool Tools for Hot Topics,
by Ron Kraybill and Evelyn Wright
El Pequeño Libro de Justicia Restaurativa, by Howard Zehr
The Little Book of Dialogue for Difficult Subjects,
by Lisa Schirch and David Campt
The Little Book of Victim Offender Conferencing,
by Lorraine Stutzman Amstutz
The Little Book of Restorative Justice for Colleges and Universities,
by David R. Karp
The Little Book of Restorative Justice for Sexual Abuse, by Judah Oudshoorn
with Michelle Jackett and Lorraine Stutzman Amstutz
*The Big Book of Restorative Justice: Four Classic Justice & Peacebuilding Books
in One Volume,* by Howard Zehr, Lorraine Stutzman Amstutz, Allan MacRae,
and Kay Pranis
The Little Book of Transformative Community Conferencing,
by David Anderson Hooker
The Little Book of Restorative Justice in Education,
by Katherine Evans and Dorothy Vaandering
The Little Book of Restorative Justice for Older Adults,
by Julie Friesen and Wendy Meek
The Little Book of Race and Restorative Justice, by Fania E. Davis
The Little Book of Racial Healing,
by Thomas Norman DeWolf, Jodie Geddes
The Little Book of Restorative Teaching Tools,
by Lindsey Pointer, Kathleen McGoey, and Haley Farrar
The Little Book of Police Youth Dialogue,
by Dr. Micah E. Johnson and Jeffrey Weisberg
The Little Book of Youth Engagement in Restorative Justice,
by Evelín Aquino, Heather Bligh Manchester, and Anita Wadhwa
The Little Book of Restorative Justice Program Design,
by Alisa Del Tufo and E. Quin Gonell
Little Book of Listening
by Sharon Browning, Donna Duffey, Fred Magondu, John A. Moore, and Patricia A. Way

The Little Books of Justice & Peacebuilding present, in highly accessible
form, key concepts and practices from the fields of restorative justice, conflict
transformation, and peacebuilding. Written by leaders in these fields, they are
designed for practitioners, students, and anyone interested in justice, peace, and
conflict resolution.

The Little Books of Justice & Peacebuilding series is a cooperative effort
between the Center for Justice and Peacebuilding of Eastern Mennonite
University and publisher Good Books.